Wittgenstein's
Tractatus

Wittgenstein's Tractatus

Translated by Daniel Kolak

The William Paterson University of New Jersey

MAYFIELD PUBLISHING COMPANY

Mountain View, California

London • Toronto

Library of Congress Cataloging-in-Publication Data
Wittgenstein, Ludwig, 1889–1951.
  [Tractatus logico-philosophicus. English]
  Wittgenstein's Tractatus / translated by Daniel Kolak.
    p.   cm.
  ISBN (invalid) 1-55934-993-4
  1. Logic, Symbolic and mathematical.   2. Language and languages—Philosophy.
I. Kolak, Daniel.   II. Title.
B3376.W563T7313   1998
192—dc21   97-34859
                                                                                               CIP

Manufactured in the United States of America.
10 9 8 7 6 5 4 3 2 1

Mayfield Publishing Company
1280 Villa Street
Mountain View, California 94041

Sponsoring editor, Ken King; production editor, Carla White; manuscript editor, Darlene Bledsoe; text designer, Donna Davis; cover designer, Joan Greenfield; cover art, © Archive Photos; art and design manager, Susan Breitbard; manufacturing manager, Randy Hurst. The text was set in 10.5/12 Adobe Garamond by Archetype Book Composition and printed on 50# Butte des Mortes by Banta Book Group, Harrisonburg.

Contents

This book is dedicated to the basement at 38

Translator's Preface

Traduttore, traditore.
　　—Nietzsche

Ludwig Wittgenstein's *Tractatus Logico-Philosophicus* is unique among the great works of philosophy. Published in the original German in 1921 and with an English translation in 1922, it was immediately heralded as a work of genius and became an instant classic. Indeed, it was viewed by many (and still is by some) as a fitting conclusion to the first three thousand years of classical philosophical inquiry: philosophy's final chapter.

Yet among all the great philosophy books, this one is the briefest. It consists of lean, terse sentences. Instead of the continuity of paragraphs, we get apocalyptic aphorisms numbered from 1 to 7, with decimal numberings for all the ones in between to mark their relative importance, spanning the entire range of philosophy—from what the world is, to logic, language, thought, knowledge, the soul, death, God, immortality, and mysticism.

My purpose is to make Wittgenstein's *Tractatus Logico-Philosophicus* accessible to today's readers. The older translations are often unnecessarily difficult, much more so than would be for the average German reading the work in the original. My translation has benefited not only from what have since become classical commentaries (especially Stenius, *Wittgenstein's Tractatus*, 1964 and Black, *A Companion to Wittgenstein's Tractatus*, 1964), but also the more recent scholarship that has brought Wittgenstein's work to a new level of clarity (especially Carruthers, *Tractorian Semantics*, 1989 and Peterson, *Wittgenstein's Early Philosophy* 1990). I have provided my own extensive commentaries (more than a hundred notes), which I have put in as endnotes. I have also rendered Wittgenstein's numerical topography into a more user-friendly graphic spacing: You can now see at a glance the relative rankings that Wittgenstein gave his sentences. Having numbered his seven main theses, Wittgenstein marks all the others as follows:

> 1.1 and 1.2, etc., are commentaries on 1, whereas 2.1 and 2.2, etc., are commentaries on 2, and so on.

> 1.11 and 1.12, etc., are commentaries on 1.1, whereas 1.21 and 1.22, etc., are commentaries on 1.2, and so on.

1.211 and 1.212 are commentaries on 1.21, whereas 1.221 and 1.222 are commentaries on 1.22, and so on.

An so on.

I have set off each level of commentary against the margin so that one can see at a glance where one is, like so:

Primary level

   Secondary level

      Tertiary level

and so on. This is a feature I think Wittgenstein might have himself incorporated.

In his author's preface, Wittgenstein suggests that the *Tractatus* "will perhaps only be understood by those who have themselves already thought the thoughts which are expressed in it—or similar thoughts." That was then. This is now.

Acknowledgments

Thanks to all the friends, colleagues, and students who in various ways helped this project, especially John White, Jaakko Hintikka, Horst Ungerer, Bill Boos, John O'Connor, Ulrich Meyer, Burton Drebin, Steve Martin, Carla White, and Ken King.

Translator's Introduction
A Tractarian Primer

Tell them I've had a wonderful life.
    —Ludwig Wittgenstein

This is a primer in the original sense as used in the fourteenth to seventeenth centuries: "a layman's prayer book containing miscellaneous prayers and psalms, used in teaching children how to read." The object of our desire is not God but Wittgenstein. The book in question is not the Bible but the *Tractatus.* These differences are insignificant.

Picasso once said, "The mark of a truly beautiful woman is that from one angle she looks so stunningly lovely you feel you will die if you cannot have her; yet, from another, she is ugly, repulsive, you are afraid of her." Such beauty borders on the sublime, in Kant's sense; it produces in us a contradiction. It transcends all categories.

The *Tractatus* is Picasso beautiful and Kant sublime. It is philosophical music in tune with Arnold Schönberg, philosophical architecture in the style of Adolf Loos. It minimizes and reveals. It clarifies and it obfuscates. It limits and expands. One loves and hates it, as Wittgenstein did. He pleaded and begged shamelessly—Frege, Russell, everybody—to help him get it published. Then, once it was published, on the flyleaf of Moritz Schlick's personal copy he wrote: *"Jeder dieser Sätze ist der Ausdruck einer Krankheit."* ("Each one of these sentences is the expression of a disease.")

Such Necker cube–like flips have become part of the book's lore. When Bertrand Russell, in his introduction, declared it an "important event in the philosophical world," C. I. Lewis wrote an angry letter to the editor of the *Journal of Philosophy:*

> Have you looked at Wittgenstein's book yet? I am much discouraged by Russell's foolishness in writing the introduction to such nonsense. I fear it will be looked upon as what symbolic logic leads to. If so, it will be the death of the subject.[1]

Except Lewis then changed his mind:

> the nature of logical truth itself has become more definitely understood, largely through the discussion of Wittgenstein.[2]

Wittgenstein too was a contradiction. The actor Dennis Hopper once described (holding up his left hand) James Dean as "the meek timidity of Montgomery Clift and [holding up his right hand] the raging force of Marlon Brando [clasping suddenly his hands together as if in prayer] fused into one genius of a contradiction." James Dean would have been the perfect actor to play Wittgenstein.[3]

Ludwig Wittgenstein (1889–1951) was born in Vienna to a prominent Jewish family that had converted to Roman Catholicism. Owners of the largest steel company in Austria, they provided the young Wittgenstein with the best tutors until the age of fourteen, when he entered the Realschule in Linz. Adolf Hitler was the same age but two years behind him in the school.[4]

Wittgenstein studied mathematics and physics. After receiving a degree in engineering in Berlin, he went to Cambridge University in England, where he met Bertrand Russell. In his autobiography Russell describes his student:

> He was perhaps the most perfect example I have ever known of genius as traditionally conceived, passionate, profound, intense, and dominating. He had a kind of purity which I have never known equaled except by G. E. Moore. . . . His life was turbulent and troubled, and his personal force was extraordinary. . . . He used to come to see me every evening at midnight, and pace up and down my room like a wild beast for three hours in agitated silence. Once I said to him: "Are you thinking about logic or about your sins?" "Both," he replied, and continued his pacing. I did not like to suggest that it was time for bed, as it seemed probable both to him and me that on leaving me he would commit suicide. At the end of his first term at Trinity, he came to me and said: "Do you think I am an absolute idiot?" I said: "Why do you want to know?" He replied: "Because if I am I shall become an aeronaut, but if I am not I shall become a philosopher." I said to him: "My dear fellow, I don't know whether you are an absolute idiot or not, but if you will write me an essay during the vacation upon any philosophical topic that interests you, I will read it and tell you." He did so, and brought it to me at the beginning of the next term. As soon as I read the first sentence, I became persuaded that he was a man of genius . . .[5]

Russell once asked G. E. Moore what he thought of Wittgenstein. Moore replied that he thought Wittgenstein was brilliant, "Because at my lectures he looks puzzled, and nobody else ever looks puzzled."

World War I interrupted Wittgenstein's studies. He left England to serve as an officer in the Austrian army. He began writing the *Tractatus* in the trenches. He completed it in an Italian prison camp. It would eventually serve as his doctoral dissertation. As the book, so the man; and as the man, so the book. The *Tractatus* gave much impetus to the antimetaphysical views of the logical positivists. Yet it can also be seen as a call to the opposite forces of mysticism. In trying to show by saying what can properly only be *shown,* Wittgenstein is doing what he claims is not strictly possible: using language to *see* beyond language. According to the *Tractatus*—because *sense* exists only within the limits of language—everything the *Tractatus* says is, therefore, strictly speaking, "nonsense." Acknowledging this contradictory nature of the work, Wittgenstein claims in the end that his book is a very special type of *illuminating* nonsense.

Consider as an analogy the story of *Flatland,*[6] about a square who lives in a two-dimensional world. One day he is enlightened by a sphere about the three-dimensional world. The square cannot see the sphere except as a two-dimensional projection into his flat, 2-D world: A circle magically appears, grows, and shrinks in and out of existence. (Think of a sphere moving through a plane.) The clever way in which the sphere enlightens the square is with the cryptic, "nonsense" phrase "upward, not northward." In the language of the square, this is strictly nonsense, for *upward* and *northward* are synonymous. That is, of the four directions of possible movement available to flatlanders, because of gravity pulling in the southward direction, "north" is "up" and "south" is "down." So when the sphere says "upward, not northward," it is like someone telling you: "Come closer but don't get any nearer." It sounds like nonsense. But in the case of the sphere talking to the square, this is not *just* nonsense but an *illuminating* sort of nonsense designed to turn his mind in the correct, *third* direction.

This allegory shows how language and thought can be limited by one's world. Indeed, it serves as a metaphor for trying to conceive of an Einsteinian world of four dimensions; as three-dimensional beings, we can't see our fourth, containing dimension, any more than the square in flatland can see the third. Relativity theory is not nonsense but a very illuminating scientific theory. In the same way, Wittgenstein's *Tractatus* can be viewed as a very illuminating theory of language to show, or at least to direct our thoughts toward, the impossible direction beyond language. Like flatlanders, we are invited to try to journey beyond the limits of our world—and to *see* what happens.

Wittgenstein's picture theory of language, sharpened by an austere tone of logical rigor, severs what can be said—sense—from what cannot be said—the mystical—with explicit statements to the effect that in the end the philosopher must remain completely silent about that which is beyond language.[7] This led the logical positivists, who wanted to bankrupt metaphysics, to welcome the *Tractatus* as their instrumental bible in the blitzkrieg against idealism in general and Hegelianism in particular. Wittgenstein, however, regarded such positivistic interpretations of his work as grossly one dimensional and claimed that they missed the essential point of his mystical allusions. (One can imagine the square in *Flatland* complaining, as he does when he is imprisoned for heresy, that he was not denying the existence of the higher but building a conceptual ladder.) Frustrated, and rightly alienated from most of the philosophers with whom he came into contact, Wittgenstein abandoned the profession in favor of teaching elementary school in the Austrian Alps. Shunning at the same time what he considered the trappings of wealth, Wittgenstein gave away his entire share of the family fortune. Thus when in time he grew disillusioned as well with teaching elementary school, he had to support himself as a gardener in a nearby monastery, taking time off to design a house for one of his sisters.

Seven years later, in 1929, Russell arranged that Wittgenstein would be awarded a doctorate in philosophy on the basis of the *Tractatus*. Wittgenstein returned to Cambridge as a lecturer. In 1937 he succeeded G. E. Moore in the chair of philosophy. He still shunned the academic life, however. He lectured mostly in his own rooms, spontaneously and without notes, in an effort to always create something new by his method of "philosophizing out loud." Although he wrote much and circulated some of it among his students, he did not allow any of it to be published during his lifetime. In 1947 he resigned from Cambridge and spent the rest of his life in seclusion, working on various unfinished manuscripts and occasionally visiting his former students.

What Is Language?

Logic is powerful; witness the computer revolution. This revolution would have been impossible without the understanding of logic and language developed by Gottlob Frege, Bertrand Russell, and Wittgenstein, whose *Tractatus* is a logical extension of their work.[8]

What did Frege and Russell do? Jacob Bronowski was once asked if he could leave but one sentence in a time bottle for future generations in case humanity's learning was ever lost, what would it be? "Everything is made of atoms." We are well enough familiar with the power unleashed by the atom— how drastically our world changed with our understanding of the atomic nature of physical matter. Russell's "logical atomism," developed from Frege's initial work, was further reduced and perfected by Wittgenstein until the full power of inner logic could be unleashed from our language. But the idea goes all the way back to Aristotle's logic. It was Aristotle who realized for the first time how much can be gained by *removing* meaning from language. What you then have is the bare form of the language, the rules by which to make transformations from one sentence, or symbolic formula, to another. The syllogism is a perfect example. For instance,

> If Smith did it, then Jones didn't do it.
> Smith did it.
> Therefore, Jones didn't do it.

This is a valid argument *not* because of anything having to do with the meanings of the words but due to the nature of the syntactical structure of the sentence formulas:

> $P \longrightarrow Q$
> P
> Therefore, Q.

Logic is in this way formal, meaning the terms of its language (P, Q, $\longrightarrow$, and so on)—by comparison to the words of informal language (*cat, table, sky,* and so on)—are *uninterpreted*. The logic as developed by Frege and Russell took the process even further, abstracting the form from the content of language. They built a new symbolism that not only revealed for the first time the complexity of the structure of relations among sentences, but gave the logician access to the underlying structure of any field of inquiry. Logic as a universal language can thus be applied to any discipline, from engineering and mathematics to theology and philosophy. It is language purified of all content—a formal, uninterpreted, purely *ideal* language.

Think, again, of minimalism in music or architecture: The power comes from revealing what ordinarily is hidden by, say, the melodic or aesthetic structures audiences enjoy; in the case of language, the meaning that ordinarily we think must be what it is all about (without which we cannot say anything) in logic gives way to syntactical formulas and symbols that seem not to say anything at all, much in the way that a Schönberg symphony may seem to be just a bunch of notes adding up to nothing.

Much of the *Tractatus* at first glance seems incomprehensible and obscure. Wittgenstein tries to create within language a new "meaningless" language for addressing philosophical concerns that can be viewed as being analogous to what in logic from Aristotle to Frege and Russell can be achieved only *outside* of ordinary language (or beneath it) with purely abstract symbolism. Thus although the *Tractatus* has all its sentences numbered like Russell and Whitehead's *Principia Mathematica,* and has the ordered structure of Frege's *Begriffsschrift,* the sentences themselves (for the most part) are not in the abstract (*formal, uninterpreted*) languages of mathematics or logic but in the (*informal, interpreted*) languages of German and English stripped by Wittgenstein of their usual meanings insofar as they are heavily colored and intoned with metaphysics. Wittgenstein strips away the usual metaphysical connotations. This is Wittgenstein's linguistic solution to the traditional metaphysical problems of philosophy.

It is stripping language of its usual metaphysical connotations that makes possible the wide latitude of interpretations for which the *Tractatus* is rightly famous, and which has led many to view it as a sort of philosophical or logical *poem.* Indeed, like many literary poets, Wittgenstein got extremely angry whenever anyone would in his presence analyze the work. During one public reading of the *Tractatus,* he began screaming at a roomful of eminent philosophers, telling them that what he had written was a poem and not meant to be butchered and dissected by them. Rudolf Carnap recalls Moritz Schlick's warning before a Vienna Circle meeting at which Wittgenstein was going to read from his work:

Before the first meeting Schlick admonished us urgently not to start a discussion of the kind to which we were accustomed in the Circle, because Wittgenstein did not want such a thing under any circumstances. We should even be cautious in asking questions, because Wittgenstein was very sensitive and easily disturbed by a direct question. The best approach, Schlick said, would be to let Wittgenstein talk and then ask only very cautiously for the necessary elucidations.[9]

What aspects of language and the world was Wittgenstein trying to evoke, express, show, in the poetic sense, through this philosophical work? "If you want to know what a mathematical theorem states," Wittgenstein advised his students, "see what its proof proves." In mathematics this is impossible without first understanding the meanings of the key terms and symbols, which often is difficult because the mathematical terms themselves defy simple and straightforward explanation. One relies in physics and mathematics on a different sort of symbolic language than ordinary language to express what ordinary language cannot express. Again, Wittgenstein in the *Tractatus* is trying to *show* what cannot be *expressed* in the language itself, not by inventing new symbols or words but by using, as far as he could, language stripped of metaphysics and pushed to its bare limits, resorting to formal (uninterpreted) symbols only when necessary.

Language according to Wittgenstein is an activity of the mind in which some parts of experience are used to represent some others. This according to Wittgenstein is also the way in which facts within the world are connected: Some facts are used as symbols to express other facts. Without this isometric correspondence between the structure of the world and the structure of language, our experience would be a Heraclitan flux. Thus it is impossible to distinguish in any *significant* way the world from the language by which the world shows itself to the mind, even though one is but a projection of the other. Here, for instance, is an isometric projection of a three-dimensional cube onto a two-dimensional plane:

Notice that one must in this case use 120-degree angles to represent 90-degree angles. To the flatlander, this would be nonsense: "a right angle of 120 degrees."

Ultimately, language and thought are one and the same; the terms are synonymous. This is so similar to the "Critical" or "Transcendental" Idealism of Immanuel Kant that we can think of Wittgenstein's Tractarian philosophy as a sort of "linguistic critical idealism." For centuries the debates among the philosophers raged about whether and to what degree the mind had access to, information about, or knowledge of reality. Materialists and rationalists tried to connect the inner mental life with the outer physical world by various theories of perception that never quite worked or left room for all sorts of errors. Idealists tried to solve the problem by in effect getting rid of the external physical world altogether and treating the mind as the only reality, using various theories that also never quite worked and were if not impossible at least very difficult to believe. Kant's brilliant solution was to come up with an "idealistic" philosophy in the very restricted sense that the *form* of experience, but *only* the form, is imposed by the mind itself upon the structure of the world. The purpose of Kant's *Critique of Pure Reason* was to set out the limits of rational inquiry and thereby move philosophy out of the empirical/rational impasse.

The belief that we experience directly some external world of things in themselves Kant called the *transcendental illusion*. Kant's key insight was that there is no way out of the illusion—that was but a pipe dream of both the rationalists and the empiricist who preceded him. Rather, transcendental illusion must be understood as what it is. This is achieved through the recognition that the phenomena in which our experience of the world consists are, in fact, not what they seem. They are, in fact, *phenomena*. This then allows us to ask the logical, purely formal question: What are the necessary conditions that make experience, as such, possible? The answer will then give us the form—the logic—of our experience. We can then use this knowledge *about the necessary limitations of knowledge* to understand ourselves and the world. What in this way Kant tries to do with the necessarily subjective nature of experience—to get at objective reality—Wittgenstein tries to do with language. According to Kant, in treating the phenomena of our experience as if they were other than phenomena—as material things in themselves (materialism) or as ideal things in themselves (idealism)—philosophers broke the rules imposed upon us by the limits of our own experience. We must therefore first get absolutely clear about those very limits of experience. Similarly, according to Wittgenstein, in treating the words of our language as though they stood for anything other than terms in our language or what is given to us in experience, we fall into the sort of transcendental error of thinking that we are dealing with what Kant called the "Noumenal" reality of things in themselves. We must therefore make perfectly clear what the limits of our language are:

> Thus the aim of the book is to set a limit to thought, or rather—not to thought, but to the expression of thoughts: for in order to be able to set a limit to thought, we should have to find both sides of the limit thinkable (i.e., we should have to be able to think what cannot be thought). It will therefore only be in language that the limit can be set, and what lies on the other side of the limit will simply be nonsense.[10]

"The *limits of any language* means the limits of my world" (5.6). The limits of the world are determined by the limits of my language.[11] Once these limits are clearly shown, the process of understanding ourselves and the world can properly begin, because we have through them attained within ourselves a certain clarity of vision *by correcting the mind's I from its tendency to look too far, to be seduced by the thought that it sees farther and more than it actually does.* It is like a corrective procedure upon a lens or mirror that doesn't add anything to language but merely removes the (metaphysical) distortion. The clarification of thought is the clarification of language. To clarify the formal structure of language becomes the Wittgensteinian process of thought clarifying itself: "The goal of philosophy is the logical clarification of thought" (4.112).

This process, however, is hardly scientific! Philosophy according to Wittgenstein should care about neither the empirical findings of science nor the discovery of everyday truths. Nor should it dwell on previously established philosophical systems: "Philosophy is not a theory but an activity" (4.112). In practical life the distinction between philosophical and scientific activity—although clear in principle—becomes confused and confuses the individual practitioners of the art. Wittgenstein charges that all traditional philosophy is a prolonged study in this confusion. His purpose in the *Tractatus* is to unconfuse these dual activities of the mind by providing the formal prerequisites of all valid thinking—that is, of all forms of symbolism—and thereby once and for all eliminate the confusion.

Recalling his advice that "If you want to know what a mathematical theorem states, see what its proof proves," let us look first at his conclusion, reflected both in his final proposition (7) "Of what we cannot speak we must be silent" and in his opening comment in his introduction that "What can be said at all can be said clearly; and whereof one cannot speak one must be silent." The upshot of this conclusion—what would be equivalent to seeing in mathematics what the "proof proves"—is that the philosopher must necessarily confine philosophical discourse to the realm of sense. The *Tractatus* therefore itself becomes the formal analysis of the *medium* of making sense: language, or symbolism in general. As Kant tried to reveal the necessary conditions that make experience possible, Wittgenstein tries to show the necessary conditions that make language possible and to which our symbolism must conform. The conditions are twofold:

1. The words of a language must have unique or unambiguous meanings, or references, to things beyond experience but *within experience.* This acquaintance must be achieved directly in experience, ostensively, by the words pointing to their designated objects. This is the philosophical *grammar.*
2. The combinations of words into sentences must make *sense.* This is determined directly in experience through the rules for combining words. This is the philosophical *syntax.*

These formal prerequisites of language cannot, however, be directly discussed in language. Because these formal prerequisites already permeate the whole of language, to do so would require our somehow standing outside of language. Now this, typically, is regarded as one of the most cryptic aspects of the *Tractatus,* but all it means is this: You cannot say something while remaining silent. To try to use language to move beyond language would be to become silent through speaking. What philosophers should do instead is therefore not to write down philosophical truths but, rather, to achieve through the verbal elucidation the realization in themselves and others of what we already know, of that which cannot be said but which nevertheless shows itself in language.

The whole of experience is of course by no means limited to thought. Thinking can in no way exhaust experience. Forever beyond thought but shown in experience is what Wittgenstein calls the *mystical.* This can be shown or expressed but cannot be the subject of any meaningful discourse in any language. Any "philosophical" discussion into those aspects of our experience that cannot be reached by words is literally nonsense, not in the good, illuminating sense but in the bad, confusing sense. According to Wittgenstein, the flaw of traditional philosophy is that it tries to breach the limitations of language to reach the realm of experience that belongs to the mystical. And the "mystical" for Wittgenstein is not some transcendental realm of reality beyond experience, but an immanent realm of reality *in* experience that is beyond the reach of language. To attempt to discuss the undiscussable is pretentious. To pretend it doesn't exist is unphilosophical.

What Is the World?

Language according to Wittgenstein is a relational process or activity in which one part of your (the subject's) experience is used to represent other parts systematically, according to fixed rules. That is how the various parts of experience fit together into what is the subject's (your) world. In this way each subject exists in its own world. Without language, each subject's experience would be utterly meaningless and nothing could be said about it for it would not constitute a system. The relation between language or thought (they are synonymous) and the world is an *internal* relation within the world of your experience and so tightly interwoven that they cannot be separated; they can, however, be discussed in abstraction, as for instance in saying that "The boundary of my language is the boundary of my world" (5.6).[12]

But what is the world? Common sense might answer: The world is the totality of things. Wittgenstein denies this. The world according to Wittgenstein is the totality not of *things* but of *facts*, and "The facts in logical space are the world" (1.13). By *logical space* Wittgenstein means the formal, grammatical structure of language. Thus in studying the grammar of my language, I am studying the formal (logical) structure of my world: "The essence of a sentence gives the essence of all description and therefore reveals the essence of the world" (5.4711). Any sentence I use has its form in common with my world.

Let us compare for a moment this view of the world with the third great influence (besides Russell and Frege) on Wittgenstein, namely, Schopenhauer:

"The world is my idea" is, like the axioms of Euclid, a proposition which everyone must recognize as true as soon as he understands it, although it is not a proposition that everyone understands as soon as he hears it. . . . among the many things that make the world so puzzling and precarious, the first and foremost is that, however immeasurable and massive it may be, its existence hangs nevertheless on a single thread; and this thread is the actual consciousness in which it exists. This condition, with which the existence of the world is irrevocably encumbered, marks it with the stamp of ideality, in spite of all empirical reality, and consequently with the stamp of the mere phenomenon. Thus the world must be recognized, from one aspect at least, as akin to a dream. For the same brain-function that conjures up during sleep a perfectly objective, perceptible, and indeed palpable world must have just as large a share in the presentation of the objective world of wakefulness. . . . the two worlds are nevertheless obviously molded from one form. This form is the intellect, the brain-function. Descartes was probably the first to attain the degree of reflection demanded by that fundamental truth; consequently, he made that truth the starting point of his philosophy . . .[13]

Wittgenstein would agree, when reading this passage from Schopenhauer, but his (pointedly nonidealistic) Fregean and Russellian standpoint would at the same time object: *Such* a statement of a thesis [to which Wittgenstein would be essentially sympathetic] does *not* have the "illuminating" properties of Tractarian nonsense. Shopenhauerian language is in Wittgenstein's view bad in that it breaches the uncrossable boundaries of language. How? By suggesting that some sort of immaterial, mind-stuff—literally, the "stuff that dreams are made of"—is the "ultimate stuff" of the world. To make *any* such *metaphysical* pronouncements is, literally, nonsense of the bad, non-illuminating variety. Wittgenstein's idea is to strip our language of all such metaphysical allusions so as to brighten our experience and our awareness of language, not to throw the mind into the illusion of moving where it cannot go, away from where the light of language is.

Clearly, for me, the conscious subject, to go "beyond" the world of my own experience, would be for me to "imagine" a totality of subjectless objects—an impossibility—and to conceive of a "real world" of (Kantian) "things in them-selves." On this point, Schopenhauer (like all nineteenth-century anti-Kantian German idealists, including Hegel, Fichte, Schelling, and Bohr[14]) and Wittgenstein would agree. But Schopenhauer (like William James's and Bertrand Russell's "neutral monism," a "radically empirical" world of "pure expe-rience") wanted to claim as much as did his mortal enemy across the hall, Hegel, that this really *is* the way the world is! In so doing Schopenhauer fails to notice that he, the subject, has inadvertently taken a God-like (impossible) point of view on the totality of language and experience. For Wittgenstein this is no less than the wasted effort of me, the subject, trying to jump out of my own intellec-tual skin. To make any such metaphysical pronouncements is the futile form of self-contradiction.

More precisely: To use a sentence that is in any way removed from the content of *my* experience or language involves the illusion that it is not interpreted from *my* perspective and is therefore neither true nor false but, literally, nonsensical. Wittgenstein, unlike Schopenhauer, Hegel, and even their former ally and subse-quent defector Russell, therefore shuns making statements about the world as it exists "in itself." Language consists not of statements about the nature of the world as it exists "in itself" but, rather, of statements showing the *restrictions* that must necessarily be imposed on any philosophical discourse, lest it be purely nonsensical noisemaking (or inkblotting). Philosophically sensible language, in other words, has tautological requirements such that *I,* the subject, give sense to my sentences within *my* experience. Language, like the formal characteristics of the world, is squarely circular, that is, universal, logical, all-encompassing, and non-metaphysical. That the world must consist of facts is a *formal* requirement of the world.

The world is complex. Language reveals this insofar as there is for me no *world* as such until *I*, the subject, coordinate the elements of my experience into the complexes that Wittgenstein calls *facts*. The particular character of the facts of which my world consists is determined by me empirically; it cannot be derived from a priori considerations, as the rationalists had imagined. "Everything we see could be other than it is. Everything we describe could be other than it is. There is no arrangement of things a priori" (5.634).

Facts are not *things* but *relations*. In language facts are mirrored by complex signs consisting of at least three entities: *a* is in some relation to *b* for *c*. One simple or atomic entity is itself meaningless until there is another entity that can be used as a sign that *means* the first. This sign must be interpreted, that is, put into a point of view, or perspective, through the isometric projection of the world that language is. This links the entities together into the elementary facts (*Sachverhalten*) of human experience that are themselves partial isometric projections of the facts (*Tatsachen*) in which the world consists. Without some such linkage, there would be no world but a purely informational inventory of individual, discrete elements. It is the (hidden) fact that my experience is a *group* (in the mathematical sense) of complexes or facts that makes possible the existence of sentences that are either true or false. Without this further (twice removed, doubly hidden) fact, *speech*, of any sort, either to oneself or to others, would be impossible. The world would be silent, literally, *absurd*. It would be "my world in which *I* do not exist."

To express a sentence, true or false, we need a complex sign—an elementary fact. Some of the sentences we use are true, others, false. This in turn requires the existence of facts in the world which the true sentences partially represent. That such facts exist is not itself a necessary condition, because there can be no necessity involved in any empirical sentence being true or false. But *unless* this is the case, the world is a purely idealistic construction in Schopenhauer's sense; true discourse in such a world would be impossible, for with the realization of the one fact alone (i.e., "The world is my idea") *we could have no world*. For the world to be a *world* (and not merely a purely verbal description of a world), that is, for there to be a space/time structure with true subject/object relations, an outside with an inside, the world *must* consist of facts.[15] Or else nothing.

To repeat: The world (*die Welt*) consists of complex facts (*Tatsachen*) that in turn consist of elementary facts (*Sachverhalten*). These elementary facts do not further consist of facts (it isn't facts "all the way down," to evoke the image of the world being held up by Atlas standing on the elephant on the turtle and then it being turtles "all the way down"). Rather, elementary facts consists of *objects* (*Gegenständen)*: "An elementary fact is a combination of objects" (2.01).

Language (formally, logically) requires that all terms have unique and unambiguous meanings (references) assigned *in the subject's own experience*. Individual words must point to their objects, an act which establishes operationally within the explicit context of the implicit universe of discourse the necessary word/object relation. In this way the meanings of words are relative to a person's use of language such that it becomes explicitly nonsensical (in the bad sense) to try to discover the "absolute" nature of one's objects of experience. Likewise, any attempt to picture or describe the nature of experience or existence in absolute terms of "things in themselves" is strictly nonsense.

One's most meaningful words are insufficient to specify a meaningful universe of discourse. Words do not a language make, any more than a "mélange of objects" conceived independently of any space makes a world.[16] Words by themselves denote their objects. Whence, then, that property of language "the language that I alone understand" [5.62]) that manifests itself in our ability of form expressions? Wittgenstein's illuminating answer is that language not just consists of sets of signals for identifying known objects, but enables the formation of expressions involving *new* combinations of objects. New facts. (*Draw* your own conclusion, literally.) This explains Wittgenstein's insistence on spontaneity in his philosophical discourse: It makes possible the activity of constructing sentences using the same old words to express *new facts*. It is literally the creation within oneself of new worlds not just for oneself but for others. (The solipsist as pantheist.[17])

Language (i.e., English, German, etc. conscripted under Tractarian philosophy[18]) is not *denotative* but *expressive,* hence the philosophical appropriateness of Wittgenstein's assertive poetical metaphors. The elementary units of language are elementary sentences, which do not themselves contain other sentences as constituents, consisting only of individual words (or symbols) in various relations: "Obviously, in analyzing sentences, we must arrive at elementary sentences consisting of names in immediate connection" (4.221). In this way epistemic completeness is made possible, insofar as a subject can in principle by knowing all the true elementary sentences have complete knowledge of its world: "The specification of all true elementary sentences describes the world completely. The world is completely described by the specification of all elementary sentences plus the specification of which ones are true and which false" (4.26); writing down all the true elementary sentences is theoretically both necessary and sufficient for a fully complete knowledge of the world. The *Tractatus* itself can be viewed as a representative set (or, I should say, a *proper class*) of such sentences for the world.[19]

What Is an Object?

What is an object? A "variable pseudoconcept," "The variable 'x' is thus the actual sign for the pseudoconcept, *object*" (4.1272). The word *object* does not stand for any specific experiential element, nor is it formed by abstraction out of experience. It is neither a general name, such as *horse* or *book,* nor a proper name, such as *Ludwig,* for some individual in the world. Well, what, then? As it turns out, there are no entities in the world itself for which the word *object* stands as a general or proper name. The word *object* does not in fact refer to anything at all in the world. What, then, is it?

An object is a symbolic device, or linguistic apparatus, for picturing genuine concepts (horse, book) or proper names such as Ludwig or even indexicals such as *this,* which do refer to something in the world. But an object is the variable, the x of $f(x)$ in an incomplete expression, a blank placeholder in a sentence that must be filled in before the sentence acquires a sense. The nature of the sentential function, the f, creates the sort of entities whose names can serve as arguments in x.

For instance, "x is blue" is a sentential function whose arguments must be some sort of spatial entities. The variable x is a symbolic device that itself but functions as a placeholder for a name or description, as in the case of "the sky is x"; it is in both cases the placeholder for a suitable adjective. In this way the object does not itself refer to or stand for any definite item in the world. In a perfect language—that is, if our symbolism could be perfect, which according to Wittgenstein is impossible—there would be no need whatsoever for symbols (words) such as *object*.

This gives us a fairly wide latitude as to how to understand objects. For instance, the ostensive reference of the word *object* can sometimes be what Wittgenstein would have construed in his formative thinking as (Russellian) sense data, as when he says that "a spot in the visual field need not be red but it must have some color: it is surrounded by color-space. Notes must have some pitch, tactile objects some degree of hardness, and so on" (2.0131). That is the sense in which objects can be seen as having a family resemblance to Humean *impressions,* about which Hume had one of this most brilliant insights when he wrote on page 2 of his *Treatise* that "By the term *impression* I would not be understood to express the manner in which our lively perceptions are produced in the soul, but merely the perceptions themselves, *for which there is no particular name either in the English or any other language, that I know of.*" Wittgenstein invented the Tractarian language for which Hume was looking and could not find.

Indeed, the open bridge to Hume is in part what inspired the logical positivist's interpretation of both Hume and Wittgenstein. Most clearly, and perhaps most importantly, the closest avatar to this line of thinking can be found in Ernst Mach's *Analysis of Sensations:* "For us . . . the world does not consist of mysterious entities, which by interaction with another, equally mysterious entity, the ego, produce sensations, which alone are accessible. For us, colors, sounds, spaces, times . . . are provisionally the ultimate elements, whose given connection it is our business to investigate."[20] Some such fundamental constituents of the world are what Wittgenstein means by *objects*.[21]

What Is Thought?

In what *sense* are the world and thought identical? In the language of idealism, for instance, thought and being are one and the same. The world and thought according to Wittgenstein are not in *that* sense identical. Language, you will recall, is according to Wittgenstein an activity in which I use some part of my experience to refer to another. What results from this activity is *my world.* Experience must be interpreted and its elements related before there is a subject in a world. Here is how this happens: "We make pictures of facts to ourselves" (2.1). The pictures we make in this way are themselves further facts:

"The picture is a fact" (2.141). It is an *interpreted* fact. Thus, "The gramophone record, the musical thought, the score, the sound waves, all stand to one another in that internal relation of depicting that holds between language and the world" (4.014). Because all such knowledge of the world arises through language in this way, there can be for *me* no other world except the world I know and I am in. There *is* for me no world except as I understand *my* world through language: *"The boundary of my language* is the boundary of my world" (5.6). Moreover, "The essence of a sentence gives the essence of all description and therefore reveals the essence of the world" (5.4711), because the sentence itself has its "essence" in common with the world.

Which parts of my experience ought I to use as symbol, and which as the symbolized? Wittgenstein's answer is that *the answer to this question is arbitrary*, purely a matter of convention usually settled by tradition, sometimes motivated by practical concerns, and sometimes purely the result of either a fortuitous or unlucky accident. What serves as symbol and what the symbol symbolizes is determined by the functional relationship between the facts and elements within the world in which the language evolves. The symbols themselves are not necessarily mental items; one can use letters or marks on a paper just as well as ideas and images.

In the world there are no fixed, predetermined, or in any sense absolute distinctions, divisions, or demarcations among the concepts *language, world,* and *thought,* at least not within the subject's own world in which any possibly relevant pseudoconcepts might arise. The downfall of both the rationalist and empiricist systems in Wittgenstein's thinking stems from the traditional (impossible) severance of (what they call *mind* and what Wittgenstein calls) *language* from *world.* Language connects the elements of our experience. Without this linguistic connection within experience, experience itself would be impossible; there would without language exist neither world nor subject.[22]

The actual world that you live in and know (and for you there can be no other), consists of objects making up elementary facts that correspond, respectively, to the meaningful terms of true elementary sentences making up your universe of discourse. Insofar as your world and my world, although no more ontologically connected than Leibnizian monads, consist not in private languages but to some degree use the same language, there is created a transworld semantics.[23] As subjects we are conjoined to our own worlds and intersubjectively to each other through the proper relation to and use of language/world relations to create the symbolic universe of reference, Wittgenstein's "great mirror." "How can the all-embracing logic that mirrors the world rely on so many special hooks and manipulations? Only because all these devices are connected into an infinitely fine network: the great mirror" (5.511).

What Is Philosophy?

Language according to Wittgenstein is a form of thought. Without thought the *objects* of thought would be sheer nonsense, meaningless pseudoevents. We might think of it this way: "The world" without it being thought about would be *tautologically meaningless.* Yet without the world there would be no such language-based activity as thinking: no thought, no language. One cannot inquire into what language is independently of the world or what the world is independent of language; to do so is to make a gross grammatical error. So, then, what question *should* the philosopher ask here?

The question is this: *What should I regard as language and what as world?* Moreover, in asking this question I must avoid any inherent tendencies to reach for broad, sweeping metaphysical generalizations. I must end where I begin: in the concrete elements of the world within which I exist as a perceiving, thinking subject. In this way I am intimately involved in the entire process from start to finish: It is *I myself* who draws the pictures of the facts in *my own world.* I can thus use language but only within the region bound by my language. I must never allow myself to think that language can in any sense be thought about as something existing apart from me and my world. (One is tempted to say: "*I* and *world* are both clothed in intention.")

"A thought is a logical picture of a fact" (3), and "A sentential sign, applied and thought, is a thought" (3.5). Moreover, "A sentence that makes sense is a thought" (4). In other words, a thought is a sentential sign used in accordance with the correct rules of language. Thinking consists in words or sentences about something in the world and is *not* necessarily mental. This is not unlike a similar view hovering around at the time, namely that of C. S. Pierce, one of the founding inventors of semiotics: "The woof and warp of all thought and all research is symbols, and the life of thought and science is the life inherent in symbols." This view has its roots in Plato, who wrote in the *Thaeatetus* that "thinking appears to me to be just talking . . . to oneself and in silence," and "thought and speech are the same with this exception that what is called thought is the *unuttered conversation.*"

The unuttered conversation is what the *Tractatus* is, except Wittgenstein takes the additional step of identifying thought with significant sentences, insofar as it involves using parts of one's experience as symbols for other parts. But in no way should thought be identified with one's psychological processes or any form of natural laws. To psychologize or naturalize Wittgenstein in this or any other similar way is unphilosophical—a mistake. For his entire view is in marked contrast to, for instance, that of John Stuart Mill, according to whom logic and mathematics are based on experience rather than the rules of symbolism as the *Tractatus* demands.

Let us take an immediate example. Right now you are thinking thoughts as you read these words. Why? Suppose we give a causal explanation: Your neurons are stimulated by the particular arrangement of inkblots on the page such that your brain makes certain neural "firings" that are then interpreted as certain noises, which are then interpreted as internal sounds, which are in turn interpreted as having a sense, and so on. What such naturalistic causal explanations fail to provide or take into account are the fundamental rules of English. We can explain all we want the causal chain from inkblots to the firing of neurons and the activities of neural nets, and so on, but, first, what explains the *rules* that make your reading of these words not just a noisy biological event but a stream of significant sentences? Second, why does your neurological system conform to these rules? Although the neurological machinery is in no way out of reach of our question here, the answer must be given not in terms of any sort of physical or even computational processes such as described by neural or computer science, nor with behaviorism, nor with *any* kind of empirical science. *To do so would be for the answer to reach beyond the question.* Rather, the answer must itself consist in terms expressive not of a theory but of the underlying *rules* by which this entire complex system runs. Your behavior as you think these thoughts follows from the rule *not because it is caused by the rule* but because it *conforms to the rule.* What guides your recognition of such rules? The answer: other rules. We must thus ultimately express the rules of both thinking and language in this way, not even with reference to experience, as in systems such as that of Mill (nor of the constructionists and intuitionists); rather, philosophical expression must in this case be formed in terms of the expressions of the rules themselves. The rules of the game are revealed to the players in the act of playing the game, through their attending to the philosophical grammar of their own activity, to thereby see as if from within themselves what is allowed and what is not. Past this point explanations cannot reach; the rules that cannot be stated must ultimately *to* the philosopher be *shown.*

Thus already inherent in Wittgenstein's thinking we see brewing the counterrevolution of his later views regarding language games. The rules of a game such as chess do not consist in empirical sentences verified by the moves made by the players. Even if no one ever played any actual game of chess, the rules would be the same (and we could not say *where* they are or *what* they are; to do so only disrupts the game). We know enough to know that the rules of the game are not psychological, physical, or any sort of natural laws of the behavior of the players: The distinction between any such *empirical* laws and *grammatical* rules is philosophically fundamental. Rules are a matter of convention, fixed in advance of the game. Laws, on the other hand, are learned through experience. In the case of language, to determine the rules means determining the proper use of the symbols, and this is done for us by the language that we exist in, quite in advance of our ever using it: "The stipulation thus concerns only the symbols, not their meaning" (3.317). In this way thought is essentially itself a form of symbolism and cannot be extracted from its context any more than a painting can be extracted from its canvas; language cannot be extracted from the world nor the world from language. Nor is thought restricted to any particular *form* of symbolism; images, objects, inkblots, pictures, computer programs—anything can be used for the signs of the language, be it physical, mental, or something else entirely. All dualisms predicated on the duality of thought and world vanish in Wittgenstein's philosophy.

How then are we to learn philosophy? We don't learn the rules of chess by observing chess players the way, say, we learn the laws of physics by studying objects rolling down inclined planes. The rules of chess and the rules of philosophy are ultimately arbitrary and set for us in advance; once we are given the primer, we must then get our lessons on the board, by playing. We must become not lofty spectators in the uppermost bleachers of the Coliseum, nor the common spectators close at hand, leaning over the edge of the wall screaming encouragements and obscenities at the players. We must become ourselves the players. We must enter the ring. We must ultimately come face-to-face, with ourselves, inside the squared circle.

And what *are* the rules? Ask me and I will strike you because you are not looking; I will have decapitated you without your knowing. One can try to formulate obscure theories to avoid playing the game or one can play the game to win. Theorizing misses the point of the question: Someone asking the question unless he or she is metaphysically challenged is asking not for a theory that gets *at* what the rules are, but rather for the rules themselves.

So how *do* we learn philosophy? There is no "getting at" any of the traditional questions of philosophy, there is only playing the philosophical game called life.

Ludwig Wittgenstein had a wonderful life.[24]

Endnotes

1. See Lewis's cover letter to his "A Pragmatic Conception of the A Priori," in *The Journal of Philosophy* 20 (1923):169–77; quoted in Burton Dreben and Juliet Floyd, "Tautology: How Not to Use a Word," *Synthese* 87(1991):23–49.

2. Quoted in Dreben and Floyd, op. cit., p. 23.

3. Wittgenstein appeared to me once in a dream, and I realized later, upon waking, that he had come in the guise of the actor James Dean; he gave me "notes" on my "performance" in the class that (in my dream) I was teaching on Wittgenstein and the logical positivists of the Vienna Circle and he was utterly disgusted with my (then, now former) lack of spontaneity; his final attack consisted of a Kripke-like pounding of fists on a poor, frightened (dream) student's desk and the bloodcurdling scream from which I (think I) awoke: "Square the circle, square the circle, you must square the circle!"

4. To grasp the full force of the world's more than occasional shocking absurdities, one need only imagine the two of them playing soccer in the schoolyard (they must have, they were the same age) and perhaps one passing the ball to the other who scores a goal and the two cheering and hugging each other. They may even have encountered each other yet again as officers and former schoolmates in the trenches of World War I, where they both served.

5. *The Autobiography of Bertrand Russell.* New York: Little Brown & Co., 1951.

6. By Edwin Abbott, reprinted in Daniel Kolak and Raymond Martin, eds., *The Experience of Philosophy,* 3rd ed. (Belmont, Calif.: Wadsworth 1996), pp. 47–65.

7. For a fuller discussion, see p. xx and pp. 26–28.

8. For a discussion of Frege and Russell, see my *From the Presocratics to the Present: A Personal Odyssey* (Mountain View, Calif.: Mayfield 1998).

9. K. T. Fann, ed., *Ludwig Wittgenstein: The Man and His Philosophy* (Harvester 1967).

10. *Tractatus,* Wittgenstein's introduction.

11. For an excellent rendition of what he calls Wittgenstein's "transcendental lingualism," see Erik Stenius, *Wittgenstein's Tractatus: A Critical Exposition of Its Main Lines of Thought* (New York: Cornell University Press 1964).

12. Wittgenstein tries to make clear the relationship between language and thought by delineating the limit of language as the expression of thought and showing how, using language, the mind is able to "hook" on to reality; language itself is the medium of representation as to how things are in the world. Just as Kant tried to show the necessary conditions that would make experiences-as-representation possible, Wittgenstein tries to show the necessary conditions that would make language-as-representation possible by claiming that the world consists ultimately not of things but of Russellian "atomic facts" made in part accessible by the propositional logic as developed by Russell. Atomic propositions are the linguistic counterparts of atomic facts, to which they are related as pictures are to the things they depict, in virtue of what Wittgenstein calls their "logical form."

13. Schopenhauer, *The World As Will and Representation*, E. F. J. Payne, trans. (New York: Dover 1996), pp. 3–6.

14. See "Chapter Four" of my *From the Presocratics to the Present*, op. cit.

15. The derivation of this involves a strange loop; it is what I like to call a *strangely synthetic a priori* judgment.

16. Think of sets first without and then with a metric, then with a topology, then a space, and then ask: What happens to the elements at the intervals?

17. Or, as I sometimes put it to my more promising students, "Since there is no way out, why not let everybody else in?"

18. I will not here speculate whether in such a case we have two languages, "English" and "Tractarian English," or one language with two expressions, one essentially expressive and one essentially denotative, or a case of semantic supervenience. I of course would opt for the latter.

19. Small wonder that its author, an impossible man at his vanishing point, realized that in its necessary incompleteness his life was sufficiently complete to be *wonderful*.

20. Mach, *The Analysis of Sensations*, in Daniel Kolak, ed., *The Mayfield Anthology of Western Philosophy* (Mountain View, Calif.: Mayfield 1998). See also the related discussions of Mach and Wittgenstein in my *From the Presocratics to the Present*, op. cit.

21. When we analyze our experience, all we find are colors, sounds, and feelings, marked by a variety of continuity and discreteness that no ordinary, denoting sentences can capture. And yet it seems that Tractarian objects sometimes are perhaps in their too polished form reflective of Whitehead's objects, Santayana's essences (which were floating around at the time), and no doubt under the austere influence of Frege, which seemed to suggest a Tractarian version of Platonic realism, as when Wittgenstein writes: "Objects form the substance of the world" (2.021) and "Substance is that which exists independently of what is the case" (2.024).

22. See my *In Search of Self: Life, Death, and Personal Identity* (Belmont, Calif.: Wadsworth, 1998).

23. What we might call a "*unified field theory of trans-world symbolic identification*." See my *In Search of Self*, op. cit.

24. Now they have been told.

Dedicated to the memory of my friend David H. Pinsent

Motto: . . . und alles, was man weiss, nicht bloss rauschen und brausen gehört hat, lässt sich in drei Worten sagen.   —KÜRNBERGER

Preface

This book will perhaps be understood only by those who have themselves already thought the thoughts which are expressed in it—or similar thoughts. It is therefore not a text-book. Its purpose would be achieved if there were one person who read it with understanding and to whom it gave pleasure.

The book deals with the problems of philosophy and shows, as I believe, that the method of formulating these problems rests on a misunderstanding of the logic of our language. Its whole meaning might be summed up as follows: What can be said at all can be said clearly; and what we cannot speak thereof we must be silent.

The book will, therefore, draw a limit to thought, or rather—not to thought, but to the expression of thought; for, in order to draw a limit to thought we should have to be able to think both sides of this limit (we should therefore have to be able to think what cannot be thought).

The limit can, therefore, only be drawn in language and what lies on the other side of the limit will be simply nonsense.

How far my efforts agree with those of other philosophers I cannot judge. Indeed what I have here written makes no claim to novelty in points of detail; and therefore I give no sources, because it makes no difference to me whether what I have thought has already been thought before me by someone else.

I will only mention that to the great works of Frege and the writings of my friend Bertrand Russell I owe for much of the stimulation of my thoughts.

If this work has a value it consists in two things. First that in it thoughts are expressed, and this value will be the greater the better the thoughts are expressed—the more the nail has been hit on the head, the greater will be its value. Here I am conscious that I have fallen far short of the possible. Simply because my powers are insufficient to cope with the task. May others come and do it better.

On the other hand the *truth* of the thoughts communicated here seems to me unassailable and definitive. I therefore believe that the problems have in essentials been finally solved. And if I am not mistaken in this, then the value of this work secondly consists in the fact that it shows how little has been achieved when these problems have been solved.

1 The world is all that is the case.

1.1 The world is the totality of facts, not of things. [1]
  1.11 The world is determined by the facts, and by these being all the facts.
  1.12 For the totality of facts determines all that is the case and also all that is not the case.
  1.13 The facts in logical space are the world.
1.2 The world can be broken down into facts.
  1.21 Each one can be the case or not be the case while all else remains the same. [2]

2 What is the case—a fact—is the existence of elementary[3] facts.[4]

  2.01 An elementary fact is a combination of objects (items, things).[5]
    2.011 It is essential that such objects[6] can be constituents of an elementary fact.
    2.012 In logic nothing is accidental: if something *can* be a constituent of an elementary fact, it must already include within itself the possibility of that elementary fact.
      2.0121 It would, so to speak, appear as an accident, if it turned out that an elementary fact[7] accommodated something that could already exist on its own.

      For something to be a constituent of an elementary fact, it must already include this possibility in itself.

      (Something logical cannot be merely possible. Logic deals with every possibility, and all possibilities are its facts.)

      Just as we cannot think of spatial objects outside space nor temporal objects outside time, so we cannot think of *any* object outside the possibility of its combining with other things.

      If I can think of an object combining with others into an elementary fact, I cannot think of it without the *possibility* of such combinations.
      2.0122 This thing [the constituting object][8] is independent [of the elementary fact] to the extent that it can occur in all *possible* elementary facts, but this form of independence is a form of connection with elementary facts and thus ultimately a form of dependence. (Words cannot appear in two different roles: by themselves, and in sentences.)

2.0123l   If I know an object, I also know all the possibilities of its occurrence in elementary facts.

(Every such possibility [what will soon be defined as *form* [9]] must lie in the nature of the object.)

New possibilities cannot be found in the future [i.e., the form cannot be altered by new possibilities discovered in the future].

2.01231   To know an object, I need not know its external [material] qualities, but I need to know all its internal [formal] properties.

2.0124   If all objects are given, then thereby are all *possible* elementary facts also given. [10]

2.013   Everything exists, as it were, in a space of possible elementary facts. I can imagine this space empty, but nothing without this space.

2.0131   A spatial object must be surrounded by an infinite space. (A point in space is a place for an argument. [11])

A spot in the visual field need not be red but it must have some color: it is surrounded by color-space. Notes must have some pitch, tactile objects some degree of hardness, and so on.

2.014   Objects contain the possibility of all elementary facts.

2.0141   The possibility of an object being part of an elementary fact is its form.

2.02   Objects are simple.

2.0201   Every complex assertion [involving compounds of objects] can be broken down into an assertion about simple constituents using sentences that describe the complex completely. [12]

2.021   Objects form the substance of the world. [13] That is why they cannot be compound.

2.0211   Were the world without substance, [14] whether one sentence made sense would depend on whether another sentence was true. [15]

2.0212   It would then be impossible to form a picture of the world (true or false).

2.022   Obviously, a world that exists only in thought, however different from the real world, must have something—a form [16]—in common with it.

2.023   This fixed form consists of objects.

2.0231   The substance of the world [17] *can* only determine such a form and not the material properties. [18] Material properties can only be presented by means of sentences—they can only be constituted by the configuration of objects.

2.0232   Roughly speaking, objects are colorless. [19]

2.0233   Two objects of the same logical form—apart from their external properties—are only distinct from one another in that they are different.

2.02331   Either a thing has unique properties, and then we can immediately distinguish it from others using a description as well as refer to it; or, on the other hand, there are several things that have a common set of all their properties, in which case it is impossible to distinguish them.

For if something is distinguished by nothing, I cannot distinguish it—otherwise it would be distinguished.

2.024 Substance is that which exists independently of what is the case.

2.025 It is form and content.

  2.0251 Space, time, and color (the state of being colored) are forms of objects.

2.026 Only if objects exist can the world have a fixed form.

2.027 The fixed, the existent, and the object are one.

  2.0271 The object is the fixed, the existent; the configuration of objects is the changing, the variable.

  2.0272 The configuration of objects forms the elementary fact.

  In an elementary fact the objects hang in one another like the links of a chain. [20]

2.03 In an elementary fact the objects hang in one another like the links of a chain.

  2.031 In an elementary fact the objects combine with one another in a definite way.

  2.032 The definite way in which objects are connected in an elementary fact is the structure of the elementary fact.

  2.033 Form is the possibility of structure.

  2.034 The structure of a fact consists of the structures of its elementary facts.

2.04 The world is a totality of all existing elementary facts.

2.05 The totality of all existing elementary facts determines which elementary facts do not exist.

2.06 The existence and nonexistence of elementary facts is reality. [21]

  (We also call the existence of elementary facts a positive fact, and their nonexistence a negative fact.)

  2.061 Elementary facts exist independently of one another.

  2.062 From the existence or nonexistence of one elementary fact we cannot infer the existence or nonexistence of any other elementary fact.

  2.063 The sum total of reality is the world.

2.1 We make pictures of facts to ourselves.

  2.11 Such a picture represents an elementary fact in logical space, the existence and nonexistence of elementary facts.

  2.12 Such a picture is a model of reality.

  2.13 To the objects correspond, [22] in such a picture, the elements of the picture.

  2.131 The picture's elements stand, [23] in the picture, for the objects.

  2.14 The picture consists in its elements being combined in a definite way. [24]

2.141 The picture is a fact.[25]

2.15 The definite way in which the picture elements combine represents how things are related.

Let us call this combination of elements[26] the *structure* of the picture, and let us call the possibility[27] of this structure the *form of representation* of the picture.

2.151 The form of representation is the possibility that things[28] combine in the same way as do the pictorial elements.

2.1511 In this way the picture makes contact with, or reaches up to, reality.

2.1512 It lays against reality like a ruler.[29]

2.15121 Only the end points of the marks on the ruler touch the object being measured.

2.1513 A picture conceived in this way includes the representing relation, which makes the picture a picture.[30]

2.1514 The representing relation consists of the correlations of picture elements with things.[31]

2.1515 These correlations are the antennae[32] of the picture's elements, which put the picture in touch with reality.

2.16 To be a picture, a fact[33] must have something in common with what it depicts.

2.161 A picture cannot depict anything unless the picture and the depicted have something identical in common.

2.17 What a picture must have in common with reality to be capable of depicting it the way it does—rightly or wrongly—is its form of representation.

2.171 A picture can represent any reality whose form it has.[34]

A spatial picture, anything spatial; a colored picture, anything colored; etc.

2.172 A picture cannot, however, depict its form of representation; it can only show it.[35]

2.173 A picture represents its subject from the outside (its point of view is its form of representation), and that is how it represents its subject rightly or wrongly.[36]

2.174 A picture cannot place itself outside its form of representation.[37]

2.18 What any such picture, of any form, must have in common with reality to be capable of representing it the way it does—rightly or wrongly—is logical form, that is, the form of reality.

2.181 A picture whose form of representation is logical is a logical picture.

2.182 Every such picture is *also* a logical picture. (Whereas, for example, every picture is not a spatial picture.)

2.19 Logical pictures are depictions of the world.

2.2 A picture must have the logical form of representation in common with what it depicts.

2.201 A picture depicts reality by representing the possible existence and nonexistence of elementary facts.

2.202 Such a picture represents a possible elementary fact in logical space.

2.203 Such a picture contains the possibility of the elementary fact that it represents.

2.21 Such a picture agrees with reality or not; it is right or wrong, true or false.

2.22 Such a picture represents what it represents independently of its truth or falsity, via its representational form.[38]

2.221 What this picture represents is its sense.

2.222 Its truth or falsity consists in the agreement or disagreement of its sense with reality.

2.223 To see whether the picture is true or false we must compare it with reality.

2.224 We cannot see whether the picture is true or false merely by looking at it.

2.225 There is no such picture that is true a priori.[39]

3 A thought is a logical picture of a fact.[40]

3.001 "An elementary fact is thinkable" means: we can form a mental picture of it.[40.1]

3.01 The totality of all true thoughts is a picture of the world.

3.02 A thought contains the possibility of the facts that it thinks. What is thinkable is also possible.

3.03 Thought cannot be of anything illogical, else we would have to think illogically.[41]

3.031 As the old saying goes: God can create anything so long as it does not contradict the laws of logic. The truth is that we could not even *say* what an illogical world might look like.

3.032 It is as impossible to say something that contradicts logic as it is to draw a figure that contradicts the laws of space or to specify the coordinates of a nonexistent point.

3.0321 An elementary fact contradicting the laws of physics can be represented spatially, but not one that contradicts the laws of geometry.

3.04 A thought that was correct a priori would ensure its truth in virtue of its possibility.

3.05 To know that a thought is true a priori you would have to recognize its truth from the thought itself (without any corresponding fact).

3.1 In a sentence the thought expresses itself perceptibly.[42]

3.11 We use a sentence (spoken or written, etc.) as a projection of a possible fact.[43]

The method of projection is our thinking the sense of the sentence.

3.12 The sign with which a thought expresses itself, I will call a sentential sign. And a sentence is a sentential sign conceived in its projective relation to the world.

3.13 The sentence has everything that the projection has, except what is projected.

Therefore, the possibility of what is projected is in the sentence, but not the projection itself.

And so the sentence does not yet contain its sense; what it does contain is the possibility of expressing that sense.

("The content of the sentence" means the content of a sentence that makes sense.)

The sentence contains the [empty, logical] form [44] of its sense, without any content.

3.14 What constitutes a sentence is that its elements, the words, stand in a determinate relation to one another.

A sentential sign is a fact.

3.141 A sentence is not merely a mixture of words. (Just as a musical theme is not merely a mixture of notes.)

A sentence is articulate. [45]

3.142 Only facts can express a sense; a class of names cannot.

3.143 That a sentential sign is a fact is concealed in its usual form of expression, whether written or printed.

For example, in a printed sentence there is no essential difference between the sentence and the word.

(Thus it was possible for Frege to call the sentence a compound name.)

3.1431 The essential nature of the sentential sign can be seen very clearly once we think of it as composed not of written signs but of spatial objects (such as tables, chairs, and books).

Then the mutual spatial layout of these objects expresses the sense of the sentence.

3.1432 We must not say, "The complex sign 'aRb' says that a stands to b in relation R," but, rather, "*That* 'a' stands to 'b' in a certain relation says *that aRb*." [46]

3.144 Facts [47] can be described but not named.

(Names are like points, sentences like arrows—they designate. [48])

3.2 In sentences, thoughts can be expressed such that the objects of the thoughts correspond [49] to the elements of the sentential signs.

3.201 I call these elements "simple signs," and such a sentence "completely analyzed."

3.202 A simple sign used in a sentence I will call a *name.*

3.203 A name signifies an object. The designated object is what the name means. [50] ("A" is the same sign as "A".)

3.21 The configuration of simple signs [51] in the sentential sign corresponds to the configuration of objects in the fact.

3.22   In a sentence a name signifies an object.

> **3.221**   Objects can only be *named.* Signs represent them. I can only speak *about* objects: I *cannot put them into words.* A sentence can only say *how* a thing is, not *what* it is.

3.23   The demand for the possibility of simple signs is the demand that sense be determinate.

3.24   A sentence about a complex stands in an internal relation to a sentence about its constituent part.

A complex can be given only by its description, which either will fit or not fit. A sentence that mentions a complex that does not exist is not meaningless, merely false.[52]

When a sentence element designates a complex, this shows up in the indeterminateness of the sentences in which it occurs.[53] We then *know* that everything is not yet determined by this sentence. (The notation for generality *contains* a prototype.)

The contraction of the symbol of a complex into a simple symbol[54] can be expressed by means of a definition.

3.25   There is one and only one complete analysis of a sentence.

> **3.251**   A sentence expresses itself clearly and distinctly: a sentence is articulate.

3.26   A name cannot be further analyzed using definitions.[55] It is a primitive sign.

> **3.261**   Every defined sign signifies *via* the signs by which it is defined; the definitions show the way.
>
> Two signs, one primitive and one defined in terms of primitive signs, cannot signify the same way. Names *cannot* be further broken down into pieces by means of definitions. (This cannot be done to any sign that signifies independently and on its own.)[56]
>
> **3.262**   What a sign fails to express gets shown by its application. What a sign conceals, its application declares.
>
> **3.263**   The meanings of primitive signs can be explained through clarifications. Clarifications are sentences containing the primitive signs. Therefore, they can only be understood when the meanings of these signs is already known.[57]

3.3   Only sentences make sense; only in the context of a sentence does a name signify anything.

> **3.31**   Any part of a sentence that characterizes the sense of the sentence I call an *expression* (a symbol).[58]
>
> (A sentence is itself an expression.)
>
> Expressions are everything essential for the sense of the sentence that sentences can have in common with each other.
>
> An expression characterizes the form and content.
>
> **3.311**   An expression presupposes the forms of all the sentences in which it can occur. It is the common characteristic mark of a class of sentences.

3.312   It therefore presents itself in the general form of the sentences that it characterizes.

And in this form the expression will be *constant* and all else *variable.*

3.313   The expression is thus presented by a variable whose values are the sentences containing the expressions.

(In the limiting case the variable becomes constant and the expression becomes a sentence.)

Such a variable I call a *sentence variable.*[59]

3.314   An expression means something only in the context of a sentence. All variables can be understood as sentence variables.

(Including variable names.)

3.315   If we turn an expression into a variable, the resulting variable sentence will have a class of sentences as its values. This class in general still depends upon what we, by arbitrary convention, mean by parts of that original sentence. But if we change all the signs whose designations have been arbitrarily turned into variables, there still always exists this type of class. This, however, is now no longer a matter of convention but depends solely on the nature of the sentence. It corresponds to a logical form—a logical prototype.[60]

3.316   The values of sentence variables are set by stipulation.

The stipulation of values *is* the variable.

3.317   Values for a sentence variable are stipulated by indicating which sentences have that variable as a common mark.

The description of those sentences is the stipulation.

The stipulation thus concerns only the symbols, not their meaning.

And all that is essential to the stipulation is *that it merely describes the symbols without stating anything about what they designate.*

The way in which we describe the sentences doesn't matter.

3.318   I conceive a sentence—like Frege and Russell—as a function of the expressions it contains.[61]

3.32   A sign is the perceptible aspect of a symbol.

3.321   Two different symbols can therefore have one and the same sign (written or spoken, etc.) in common—in which case each will signify in a different way.

3.322   Using the same sign to signify two different objects can never show a common characteristic. For the sign is of course arbitrary. So we could instead choose two different signs, and then where would there be what was common in the symbolization?

3.323   In ordinary language it often happens that the same word signifies in two different ways—and therefore belongs to two different symbols—or that two words, which signify in different ways, are apparently applied in the same way in the sentence.

Thus the word "is" appears as a copula, as a sign for identity, and as an expression for existence; "exist" appears as an intransitive verb, like "go"; and "identical" appears as an adjective; we speak of *something*, and also of *something* happening.

(In the sentence, "Green is green"—where the first word is a proper name and the last an adjective—not only do these words have different meanings, they are *different symbols*.)

3.324 This is how the most fundamental confusions can easily arise (philosophy is full of them).

3.325 To avoid such errors we must employ a symbolic language that excludes them, by never applying the same sign in different symbols and by not applying signs in the same way that signify in different ways: a symbolic language, that is to say, that obeys the rules of *logical* grammar—of logical syntax.

(The logical symbolism of Frege and Russell is such a language that, however, still does not exclude all errors.)

3.326 To recognize a symbol by its sign we must observe the sense in which it is used.

3.327 The sign determines a logical form only together with its use according to logical syntax.

3.328 An unused sign is meaningless. That is the point of Occam's razor.

(When everything behaves as if a sign has meaning, that sign does have a meaning.)

3.33 The meaning of a sign should never play a role in logical syntax. It must be possible to formulate logical syntax without mentioning the *meaning* of a sign; it ought *only* to presuppose the description of the expressions.

3.331 From this observation we get a comprehensive view of Russell's "theory of types" and can see Russell's mistake: in drawing up his symbolic rules, he had to speak about the things his signs mean.

3.332 No sentence can assert anything about itself, because a sentence cannot be contained in itself (that is the essence of the "theory of types").

3.333 A function cannot be its own argument because the sign for a function already contains the prototype of its argument, and so cannot contain itself.

If, for example, we suppose that the function $F(fx)$ could be its own argument, there would then be a sentence "$F(F(fx))$" in which case the outer function F and inner function F must have different meanings; for the inner has the form $\phi(fx)$ and the outer one has the form $\psi(\phi(fx))$. The two functions have only the letter "F" in common, which by itself signifies nothing.

This is immediately clear if instead of "$F(F(fu))$" we write "$(\exists\phi):F(\phi u).\phi u = Fu$".

Hereby Russell's paradox vanishes.

3.334 All the rules of logical syntax become self-evident once we know how every single sign signifies.

3.34 A sentence has essential and accidental features.

The accidental features arise in the way the sentence is produced, the essential features are the ones without which the sense of the sentence would be lost.

3.341 What is essential about a sentence is what all sentences that can express the same sense have in common.

Likewise, generally, what is essential about a symbol is what all symbols capable of fulfilling the same function have in common.

3.3411 So one could therefore say that the real name is that which all symbols that signify an object have in common. It would then follow, step by step, that no sort of composition at all would turn out to be essential to the name.

3.342 In our notations there is indeed something arbitrary, but *this* is not arbitrary; namely, that *if* we have determined anything arbitrarily, then something else *must* necessarily be the case. (This results from the *essence* of the notation.)

3.3421 A particular method of symbolizing may be unimportant, but that it is a *possible* way of symbolizing is always important. And that's the way it often goes in philosophy: again and again the particular detail turns out to be unimportant, whereas the possibility of each detail discloses something essential about the world.

3.343 Definitions are rules for the translation of one language into another. Every correct symbolism must be translatable into every other according to such rules. *This* is what they all have in common.

3.344 A symbol signifies in virtue of what is common to all those symbols by which it can be replaced according to the rules of logical syntax.

3.3441 Here is how we can express what is common to all notations for truth-functions: for instance, it is common to them that they all *can be replaced* by the notations of "~p" ("not p") and "p v q" ("p or q").

(This indicates the way in which a special possible notation can supply us with general information.)

3.3442 The sign of a complex cannot be arbitrarily resolved in the analysis in such a way that its resolution would be different in every sentential structure.

3.4 A sentence determines a place in logical space. The existence of this logical place is guaranteed by the existence of the expressions of which the sentence is composed—by the existence of the meaningful sentence.

3.41 The sentential sign with logical coordinates: that is the logical place.

3.411 Both in geometry and in logic, a place is a possibility: something can exist in it.

3.42 Although a sentence may determine only one place in logical space, the whole logical space must already be given by it.

(Otherwise negation, logical sum, logical product, etc., would always introduce new elements—in coordination.)

(The logical scaffolding around the picture determines the whole logical space. The sentence reaches through the whole logical space.)

3.5   A sentential sign, applied and thought, is a thought.

4 A sentence that makes sense is a thought.[62]

>   **4.001**   The totality of sentences is the language.
>
>   **4.002**   Human beings possess the capacity of constructing languages in which every sense can be expressed without our having any idea how and what each word means, just as we speak without knowing how the individual sounds are produced.
>
>   Ordinary language is a part of the human organism and no less complicated than it.
>
>   It is humanly impossible to gather from it the logic of language.
>
>   Language disguises thought, so that from the external form of the clothes one cannot infer the form of the thought beneath, because the external form of the clothes is designed not to reveal the form of the body but for different purposes.
>
>   The silent adjustments to understand ordinary language are extremely complicated.
>
>   **4.003**   Most of the statements and questions found in philosophy are not false but nonsensical. We cannot, therefore, answer such questions at all but only show them to be nonsensical. Most questions and statements of the philosophers result from our inability to understand the logic of our language.
>
>   (They are of the same variety as the question, "Is the Good more or less identical than the Beautiful?")[63]
>
>   No wonder that the deepest problems are actually *not* problems.
>
>   >   **4.0031**   All philosophy is a "critique of language." (But not at all in Mauthner's sense.[64]) Russell's merit is to have shown that the apparent logical form of a sentence need not be its real form.
>
>   **4.01**   A sentence is a picture of reality.
>
>   A sentence is a model of reality as we think it is.
>
>   **4.011**   At first glance a sentence—say as it is laid out on the printed page—does not seem to be a picture of the reality that it is about. But neither does the musical score appear at first glance to be a picture of a musical piece; nor does our phonetic spelling (the letters of the alphabet) seem to be a picture of our spoken language. And yet these symbolisms turn out to be pictures—even in the ordinary sense of the word—of what they represent.
>
>   **4.012**   Obviously, a sentence of the form "$a\mathcal{R}b$" looks like a picture. Here the sign is obviously a likeness of what is signified.

4.013   And if we penetrate into the essence of this visualization, we see that it is not hindered by *apparent irregularities* (such as the use of ♯'s and ♭'s in musical notation).

For even these irregularities depict what they are to express, only in a different way.

4.014   The gramophone record, the musical thought, the score, the sound waves, all stand to one another in that internal relation of depicting that holds between language and the world.

They all have the logical structure in common.

(Like the two youths, their two horses, and their lilies in the fairy tale. In a certain sense they are all one.)

4.0141   In the fact that there is a general rule by which the musician is able to read the symphony from the score, and that there is a rule by which one can reconstruct the symphony from the grooves in the gramophone record and from this again—by means of the first rule—construct the score, herein lies the internal similarity between these things that at first glance seem so completely different. And the rule is the law of projection that projects the symphony into the language of the musical score. It is the rule of translation of this language into the language of the gramophone record.

4.015   The possibility of all similes, of all the imagery of our language, rests on the logic of representation.

4.016   To understand the essential nature of a sentence, consider hieroglyphic writing, which pictures the facts it describes.

And from it came the alphabet without the essence of the representation being lost.

4.02   This we see from the fact that we understand the sense of a sentence without having had it explained to us.

4.021   A sentence is a picture of reality, for if I understand the sentence, I know the fact represented by it. And I understand the sentence without its sense having been explained to me.

4.022   A sentence *shows* its sense.

A sentence *shows* how things are *if* it is true. And it *says* that that is how they are.

4.023   A sentence determines reality to the degree that one only needs to say "yes" or "no" to it, and nothing more, to make it agree with reality.

Reality must therefore be completely described by the sentence.

A sentence is the description of a fact.

Just as a description describes an object by its external properties, so a sentence describes reality by its internal properties.

A sentence constructs a world with the help of a logical scaffolding, so that one can actually see in the sentence all the logical features of reality *if* it is true. One can *draw conclusions* from a false sentence.

4.024 To understand a sentence means to know what is the case if it is true.

(One therefore understands it independently of knowing whether it is true.)

One understands the sentence if one understands its expressions.

4.025 The translation of one language into another is not a process of translating each sentence of one language into a sentence of the other language but only the constituent parts.

(And the dictionary translates not only substantives but also adverbs and conjunctions, etc., and it treats them all alike.)

4.026 The meanings of simple signs (the words) must be explained to us before we can understand them.

By means of sentences we explain ourselves.

4.027 It is essential to sentences that they can communicate a new sense to us.

4.03 A sentence must communicate a new sense with old words.

A sentence communicates a fact to us, therefore it must be *essentially* connected with the fact.

And the connection is that it is its logical picture.

A sentence asserts something only insofar as it is a picture.

4.031 In a sentence the fact is, as it were, put together as an experiment.

Instead of saying "The sense of this sentence is such and such," we can say, "This sentence represents such and such a fact."

4.0311 One name stands for one thing, and another for another, and they are connected together. And so the whole—like a *tableau vivant* [living picture]⁶⁵—presents an elementary fact.

4.0312 The possibility of sentences is based upon the principle that things are represented by their signs.

My fundamental thought is that the "logical constants" do not represent anything, that the *logic* of the facts cannot be represented.

4.032 A sentence is a picture of its fact only insofar as it is logically articulated.

(Even the sentence "ambulo" is composite, for with a different ending its stem yields a different sense, as does its ending with a different stem.)

4.04 In a sentence there must be exactly as many things distinguishable as there are in the fact that it represents.

They must both possess the same logical (mathematical) multiplicity. (Compare Hertz's *Mechanics* on dynamic models.)

4.041 Naturally, this mathematical multiplicity cannot itself be represented.⁶⁶ Yet one cannot miss it in the representation.

4.0411 Say we wanted to express what is expressed by "$(x).f(x)$" by putting an index in front of "fx", like: "$Gen.fx$", it simply would not do, for we would not know what was generalized. If we tried to show by an index "ₘ", like: "$f(x_g)$", it still would not do, for we would not know the scope of the generalization.

Suppose we tried to do it by introducing a mark into the argument places, like

$$(G,G).F(G,G)",$$

it would not do: we could not determine the identity of the variables, etc.

All these ways of symbolizing are inadequate because they do not have the requisite mathematical multiplicity.

4.0412   Likewise, the idealist explanation of the seeing of spatial relations through "spatial glasses" does not work, because it cannot explain the multiplicity of these relations.[67]

4.05   The reality is compared with the sentence.

4.06   Sentences can be true or false only by being pictures of the reality.

4.061   If one does not notice that sentences make sense independently of the facts, one can easily believe that true and false are relations of equal value between signs and what the signs represent.

One could then say, for instance, that "p" truly signifies what "$\sim p$" falsely signifies, etc.

4.062   Can we not make ourselves understood by means of false sentences just as we have done up to now with true ones, so long as we know that they are meant to be false? No! For a sentence is true when what it asserts is the case; and if by "p" we mean "$\sim p$" and that's what is the case, then "p" in the new conception is true and not false.

4.0621   But it is important that the signs "p" and "$\sim p$" *can* say the same thing. For it shows that the sign "$\sim$" corresponds to nothing in reality.

That negation occurs in a sentence is not enough to characterize its sense ($\sim\sim p = p$).

The sentences "p" and "$\sim p$" have opposite senses, but one and the same reality corresponds to them.

4.063   Here is an analogy to illustrate the concept of truth. A black spot on white paper; the form of the spot can be described by saying for each point on the sheet whether it is black or white. To the fact that some point is black corresponds a positive fact, and to the fact that some point is white (not black) corresponds a negative fact. If I indicate a point on the sheet (a Fregean truth-value) this corresponds to the supposition presented for judgment, etc., etc.

However, to be able to say whether a point is black or white, I must first know under what conditions a point is called white or black; I cannot say "p" is true (or false), unless I know in advance the circumstances in which "p" is called true, and in so doing I determine the sense of the sentence.

The point at which this simile breaks down is this: we can still pick a point on the paper even if we don't know what black and white are; but to a sentence that does not make sense, there corresponds nothing at all, for it signifies nothing (a truth-value) whose properties are called "false" or "true"; the verb of the sentence is not "is true" or "is false," as Frege thought, but that which "is true" must already contain the verb.

4.064 Every sentence must *already* have a sense; assertion cannot give it a sense, for what it asserts is the sense itself. The same goes for negation, etc.

4.0641 One can say: the negation must already be related to the logical place determined by the negated sentence.

The negating sentence determines a *different* logical place from the negated sentence.

The negating sentence determines a logical place using the logical place of the negated sentence by describing it as lying outside its logical place.

That the negated sentence can again be negated shows that what is negated is already a sentence and not just something assumed in advance of the sentence.

4.1 A sentence presents the existence and nonexistence of elementary facts.

4.11 The totality of true sentences is the whole of natural science (or the totality of the natural sciences).

4.111 Philosophy is not one of the natural sciences.

(The word "philosophy" must mean something that stands above and below the natural sciences, not alongside them.)

4.112 The goal of philosophy is the logical clarification of thought.

Philosophy is not a theory but an activity.

A philosophical work consists essentially of clarifications.

The end result of philosophy is not a number of "philosophical sentences" but to make sentences clear.

Philosophy should make clear and sharpen the contrast of thoughts that are otherwise opaque and blurred.

4.1121 Psychology is no more related to philosophy than is any other natural science.

The theory of knowledge is the philosophy of psychology.

Does not my study of symbolism correspond to the study of thought processes that philosophers have held to be so essential to the philosophy of logic? Only they got involved for the most part in inessential psychological investigations, and there is an analogous danger with my method.

4.1122 The Darwinian theory has nothing to do with philosophy, any more than does any hypothesis in the natural sciences.

4.113 Philosophy limits the domain of natural science.

4.114 It must limit the thinkable and thereby the unthinkable.

It must limit the unthinkable from within through the thinkable.

4.115   It will show what cannot be said by clearly presenting all that can be said.

4.116   Everything that can be thought at all can be thought clearly. Everything that can be said can be said clearly.

4.12   Sentences can represent the whole reality, but they cannot represent what they must have in common with reality to be able to represent it—the logical form.

To be able to represent logical form, we would have to be able to place ourselves with sentences outside logic, that is, outside the world.

4.121   Sentences cannot represent the logical form; the logical form mirrors itself in the sentences.

Language reflects what it cannot represent.

That which expresses *itself* in language, *we* cannot express by means of language.

Sentences *show* the logical form of reality.

They exhibit it.

4.1211   Thus a sentence "fa" shows it is about a, two sentences "fa" and "ga" show they are about the same object.

If two sentences contradict each other, their structure shows it; likewise, if one of them implies the other. And so on.

4.1212   What *can* be shown *cannot* be said.

4.1213   Now we understand our feeling that we possess the right logical conception, if only all is right in our symbolism.

4.122   In some sense we can talk about formal properties of objects and elementary facts, or about the structural properties of facts and about relations of form and restructure.

(Instead of "structural property" I can just as well say "internal property"; instead of "structural relation," "internal relation." I introduce these expressions to show the reason for the confusion between internal relations and proper (external) relations, so common among philosophers.)

However, one cannot use sentences to assert such internal properties and relations; rather, this shows itself in the sentences that present the relevant facts and objects in question.

4.1221   An internal property of a fact can be called a feature of that fact (in the sense that we speak of facial features).

4.123   A property is internal if it is logically impossible for its object to not possess it.

(One shade of blue and another stand, *eo ipso,* in the internal relation of lighter to darker. It is logically inconceivable that those two objects could not be related in this fashion.)

(Here to the shifting use of the words "property" and "relation" there corresponds the shifting use of the word "object.")

4.124   The internal property of a possible fact cannot be expressed using sentences; rather, it shows *itself* in the sentence that presents the statement, by means of an internal property of that sentence.

It would be as nonsensical to ascribe a formal property to a sentence as to deny it the formal property.

4.1241 Forms cannot be distinguished from one another by saying that one has this or that property and the other does not, for this presupposes that either property can be ascribed to either form.

4.125 That an internal relation holds between possible facts expresses itself in language by means of the internal relation that holds between the sentences that present them.

4.1251 Now this settles the disputed question,[68] "Are all relations internal or external?"

4.1252 A series ordered by an *internal* relation I call a formal series.

The number series is governed not by an external relation but by an internal one.

The same holds of the series of sentences

"aRb"

"$(\exists x):aRx.xRb$"

"$(\exists x,y):aRx.xRy.yRb$",

and so on.

(If b is related to a in one of these ways, I call b a successor of a.)

4.126 In the same sense that we can speak of formal properties, we can now speak of formal concepts.

(I introduce this expression to show the source of confusion between formal concepts and proper concepts, which infects all of traditional logic.)

Something's being an instance of a formal concept cannot be expressed by a sentence but is shown in the sign for that object. (The name shows that it designates an object, the numeral that it designates a number, etc.)

Unlike actual concepts, formal concepts cannot be presented by a function.

This is because their marks—formal properties—cannot be expressed using functions.

The expression of a formal property is an internal property of certain symbols.

A mark of a formal concept is symbolized by a distinctive internal property of all sentences that include instances of the concept.

The expression of a formal concept is a sentential variable in which this distinctive internal property alone is constant.

4.127 The sentential variable signifies the formal concept and its values signify the objects that are its instances.

4.1271 Each variable is a sign for a formal concept.

Each variable represents the constant form of its values, which can be viewed as the formal properties of the values.

4.1272 The variable name "x" is thus the actual sign for the pseudo-concept,[69] *object*.

Whenever the word "object" ("thing," etc.) is used correctly, it is expressed by a variable name in conceptual notation.

For instance, in the sentence "There exist 2 objects that . . . ," it is expressed by "$(\exists x, y)$. . . ."

Used as an actual concept-word, it creates nonsensical pseudo-sentences.[70]

Thus for instance we cannot say "There are objects," in the way we say "There are books." And it is equally impossible to say "There are 100 objects" or "There are $\aleph$ objects."

And it makes no sense to speak of the *total number of objects.*[71]

This also applies to words like "complex," "fact," "function," "number," etc.

These all refer to formal concepts and are represented in conceptual notation not by functions or classes (as Frege and Russell believed) but by variables.

"1 is a number," "There is only one zero," and all similar expressions are nonsense.[72]

(To say "There is only one 1," "2+2 at 3 o'clock equals 4," would be equally nonsense.)[73]

4.12721   The formal concept is already given by an object that is an instance of the formal concept. Therefore it is impossible to introduce as primitive ideas both the formal concept and the objects that are instances of it. For example, one cannot introduce as primitive ideas both the concept of a function and specific functions, as Russell does, or the concept of a number along with particular numbers.

4.1273   To express the general sentence "*b* is a successor of *a*" in logical notation, we need an expression for the general term of the formal series

"aRb"

"$(\exists x):aRx.xRb$"

"$(\exists x,y):aRx.xRy.yRb$",

. . .

To express a general term of a formal series, we must use a variable because the concept "term of the formal series" is itself a *formal* concept. (This is what Frege and Russell overlooked; their way of expressing such general sentences is wrong; it contains a vicious circle.)

We can determine the general term of a formal series by stating its first term along with the general form of the operation by which the next term can be produced out of the preceding sentence.

4.1274   It makes no sense to ask whether a formal concept exists. For there is no sentence that could possibly answer this question.

(For example, one cannot ask, "Are there unanalysable subject-predicate sentences?")

4.128 Logical forms are uncountable.[74]

Therefore, in logic there are no preeminent[75] numbers, and therefore there is no philosophical monism or dualism, etc.

4.2 The sense of a sentence is in its agreement and disagreement with the possibilities of the existence and nonexistence of elementary facts.

4.21 The simplest sentence, the elementary sentence, asserts the existence of an elementary fact.

4.211 It is a characteristic of an elementary sentence that no elementary sentence can contradict it.

4.22 An elementary sentence consists of names. It is a connection, a linkage of names.

4.221 Obviously, in analyzing sentences, we must arrive at elementary sentences consisting of names in immediate connection.

This raises the question of how such sentential connections arise.

4.2211 Even if the world is infinitely complex, so that every fact consists of infinitely many elementary facts and every elementary fact consists of infinitely many objects, even so there must be objects and elementary facts.

4.23 A name occurs in a sentence only in the context of an elementary sentence.

4.24 Names are the simplest symbols, and so I indicate them by single letters ("x", "y", "z").

An elementary sentence I write as a function of names in the form "$f(x)$", "$\phi(x,y)$", etc.

Or I indicate it by the letters "p", "q", "r".

4.241 When I use two different signs to signify one and the same object, I indicate this by placing the sign "$=$" between them.

Thus, "$a = b$" means that the sign "b" can be substituted for the sign "a".[76]

(If I use an equation to introduce a new sign "b", saying that this will be a substitute for some already known sign "a", then (like Russell) I write the definition of the equation in the form "$a = b$ Def". A definition is a rule about signs.)

4.242 Expressions having the form "$a = b$" are merely expedient aids in presentation; they assert nothing about the significations of the signs "a" and "b".

4.243 Can we understand two names unless we know whether they signify the same object or two different objects? Can we understand a sentence containing two names without knowing whether they signify the same thing or not?

If I know that an English word and a German word signify the same thing,[77] then it is impossible for me not to know that they are synonymous, it is impossible for me not to be able to translate them into one another.

Expressions like "$a=a$", and others derived from them, are not elementary sentences, nor is there any other way in which they could make sense. (This will be shown later.)

4.25 If the elementary sentence is true, the elementary fact exists; if the elementary sentence is false, the elementary fact does not exist.

4.26 The specification of all true elementary sentences describes the world completely. The world is completely described by the specification of all elementary sentences plus the specification of which ones are true and which false.

4.27 With respect to the existence and nonexistence of n elementary facts, there are

$$Kn = \sum_{v=0}^{n} \binom{n}{v}$$

possibilities.

It is possible for all combinations of elementary facts to exist, and for the others not to exist.

4.28 To these combinations correspond an equal number of possibilities of truth—and falsehood—for n elementary sentences.

4.3 Truth-possibilities of elementary sentences signify the possibilities of the existence and nonexistence of elementary facts.[78]

4.31 We can show truth-possibilities by the following sort of schemata ("T" means "true," "F" means "false"; the columns of T's and F's under the row of elementary sentences symbolize their truth-possibilities perspicuously):

p	q	r
T	T	T
F	T	T
T	F	T
T	T	F
F	F	T
F	T	F
T	F	F
F	F	F

p	q
T	T
F	T
T	F
F	F

p
T
F

4.4 A sentence is an expression of agreement and disagreement with the truth-possibilities of elementary sentences.[79]

4.41 The truth-possibilities of elementary sentences are the conditions of the truth and falsehood of the sentence.

4.411 It is likely that the introduction of the elementary sentences provides the foundation for understanding all other kinds of sentences. Indeed, understanding general sentences *obviously* depends on understanding the elementary sentences.

4.42 With respect to the agreement and disagreement of a sentence with the truth-possibilities of *n* elementary sentences, there are

$$\sum_{k=0}^{Kn} \left(\frac{K}{k}\right) = Ln$$

possibilities.

4.43 Agreement with truth-possibilities can be expressed by correlating the mark "T" (true) with them in the schema.

The absence of this mark means disagreement.

4.431 Formulation of the truth-possibilities of the elementary sentences expresses the truth-conditions of the sentence.

The sentence is the expression of its truth-conditions.

(Frege was therefore right to put them at the beginning, as explaining the signs of his *Begriffsschrift* [logical notation]. But Frege's explanation of the concept of truth is false: if "the true" and "the false" were real objects and the arguments in ~p, etc., then the sense of "~p" would in no way be determined by Frege's determination.)

4.44 The sign resulting from the correlation of the mark "T" with the truth-possibilities is a sentential sign.[80]

4.441 Clearly, a complex of the signs "F" and "T" has no corresponding object (or complex of objects), just as no objects correspond to the horizontal and vertical lines [as in 4.31] or to the brackets [as in 5.461]. There are no "logical objects."

Naturally, the same applies to all signs expressing what is expressed by the schemata of T's and F's.

4.442 For instance, the following is a sentential sign:

" *p*	*q*	
T	T	T
F	T	T
T	F	
F	F	T "

(Frege's assertion sign "⊢" is logically altogether meaningless: in Frege (and in Russell) it only shows that these authors hold as true the sentences marked in this way. "⊢" belongs as little to the sentences as their number. A sentence cannot possibly assert of itself that it is true.)

If the sequence of the truth-possibilities in the schema is fixed by a rule of combination, then the last column is by itself an expression of the truth-conditions. Writing this column as a row, the sentence becomes:

"(TT-T)(*p,q*)"   or, more clearly   "(TTFT)(*p,q*)".

(The number of terms in the right-hand pair determines the number of places in the left-hand pair.)

4.45 For n elementary sentences, there are L_n possible groups of truth-conditions.

The groups of truth-conditions that belong to the truth-possibilities of a given number of elementary sentences can be ordered into a series.

4.46 Among the possible groups of truth-conditions are two limiting cases.

In one case the sentence is true for all the truth-possibilities of the elementary sentences: the truth conditions are *tautological.*

In the second case the sentence is false for all truth-possibilities: the truth-conditions are *self-contradictory.*

In the first case we call the sentence a tautology; in the second case we call it a contradiction.

4.461 A sentence shows what it says; a tautology and a contradiction show that they say nothing.

Because a tautology is true unconditionally, it has no truth-conditions; likewise, on no condition is a contradiction true.

Tautologies and contradictions do not make any sense.

(Like a point with two arrows emerging in opposite directions.)

(For example, in knowing that it is either raining or not raining, I know nothing about the weather.)

4.4611 However, neither are tautologies nor contradictions non-sensical. They belong to the symbolism, just as "0" belongs to the symbolism of arithmetic.

4.462 Tautologies and contradictions are not pictures of the reality. They present no possible facts. For tautologies admit *all* possible facts, and contradictions admit *none.*

In the tautology the conditions of agreement with the world—the presenting relations—cancel each other out, so that in the tautology no aspect of reality can present itself.

4.463 The truth-conditions of a sentence determine the play[81] left to the facts.

(The sentence, the picture, the model are in a negative sense like a solid body, which restricts the free movement of another; in a positive sense, they are like a bound space into which a body may be placed.)

A tautology leaves the whole infinite logical space open to reality; a contradiction fills in the whole logical space, leaving no point to reality. Thus neither of them can determine reality in any way.

4.464 The truth of tautology is certain, that of sentences possible, and that of contradiction impossible.

(Certain, possible, impossible: here we have a hint of the gradation needed in probability theory.)

4.465 The logical product of a tautology and a sentence[82] says the same thing as the sentence. This logical product is therefore identical with the sentence. For the essence of a symbol cannot be altered without altering its sense.

4.466   A definite logical combination of signs corresponds to a definite logical combination of the objects signified by the signs (their semantic content).[83]

That is, sentences that are true for every fact [i.e., tautologies] cannot be combinations of signs at all, for otherwise only particular combinations of objects would correspond to them.

(And there isn't any logical combination to which there corresponds *no* combination of the designated objects.)

Tautology and contradiction are the limiting cases of the combinations of signs, their point of disintegration.[84]

4.4661   Of course the signs are still combined even in tautologies—that is, they stand in certain relations to one another, but these relations are meaningless, in no way are they essential to the symbol.

4.5   We are in a position now to state the most general form of a sentence—that is, to describe the sentence of any symbolic language whatsoever such that every sense can be expressed by a symbol satisfying the description and every symbol satisfying the description can express a sense, provided that the signification of each name is well chosen.

Clearly, only what is essential to the most general form of a sentence may be included in its description—otherwise, it would not be the most general form.

The existence of a general form of a sentence is proved in that no sentence can be given whose form could not have been foreseen (i.e., constructed). The general form of a sentence is soandso[85] is the case.

4.51   Suppose *all* elementary sentences were given me: then we can simply ask what sentences I can build out of them. And these are *all* the sentences and *that* is how they are bound.

4.52   Sentences are all that follows from the totality of elementary sentences (and of course from its being the *totality of them all*). (Thus we might say that in a certain sense *all* sentences are generalizations of elementary sentences.)

4.53   The general form of a sentence is a variable.[86]

5 A sentence is a truth-function of elementary sentences.[87]

(An elementary sentence is a truth-function of itself.)

5.01   Elementary sentences are the truth-arguments of sentences.

5.02   It is quite natural to confuse the arguments of functions with the indices of names. For I recognize equally well from the argument and from the index what is meant by the signs containing them.

In Russell's "$+_c$", for instance, "c" is an index indicating that the whole sign is the addition-sign for cardinal numbers.[88] But this way of symbolizing is an arbitrary convention, and we could have chosen a simple sign instead of "+c". In "~p", on the other hand, "p" is not an index but an argument: the sense of "~p" *cannot* be understood unless one already understands the sense of "p". (In the name Julius Caesar, "Julius" is an index. The index is always part of the description of the designated object to whose name we attach it, for example, *the* Caesar of the Julius gens.)

The confusion of argument and index stems, unless I am mistaken, from Frege's theory about the meaning of sentences and functions. For Frege, the sentences of logic are names and their arguments are the indices of these names.

5.1   The truth-functions can be ordered in a series.

This is the foundation for the theory of probability.

> **5.101**   The truth-functions of every number of elementary sentences can be arranged in the following sort of schema:
>
> (TTTT)(p,q) Tautology (if p then p, and if q then q)   [$p{\supset}p. \ q{\supset}q$]
> (FTTT)(p,q) in words : Not both p and q.   [~($p. \ q$)]
> (TFTT)(p,q)   "   "   If q then p.   [$q{\supset}p$]
> (TTFT)(p,q)   "   "   If p then q.   [$p{\supset}q$]
> (TTTF)(p,q)   "   " p or q.   [$p{\vee}q$]
> (FFTT)(p,q)   "   "   Not q.   [~q]
> (FTFT)(p,q)   "   "   Not p.   [~p]
> (FTTF)(p,q)   "   " p or q, but not both.   [$p. \sim q : \vee : q. \sim p$]
> (TFFT)(p,q)   "   "   If p, then q; and if q, then p.   [$p{\equiv}q$]
> (TFTF)(p,q)   "   " p
> (TTFF)(p,q)   "   " q
> (FFFT)(p,q)   "   "   Neither p nor q.   [~$p. \sim q$ or $p|q$]
> (FFTF)(p,q)   "   " p and not q.   [$p. \sim q$]
> (FTFF)(p,q)   "   " q and not p.   [$q. \sim p$]
> (TFFF)(p,q)   "   " p and q.   [$p.q$]
> (FFFF)(p,q) Contradiction (p and not p; and q and not q.)[$p. \sim p.q. \sim q$]

The truth-possibilities of a sentence's truth-arguments that make the sentence true I shall call its *truth-grounds*.

5.11   If the truth-grounds common to several sentences are also the truth-grounds of some one sentence, then we say that the truth of that sentence follows from the truth-grounds of the others.

5.12   In particular, the truth of a sentence "p" follows from the truth of a sentence "q" if all the truth-grounds of "q" are the truth-grounds "p".

> **5.121**   The truth-grounds of q are extracted from[89] the truth-grounds of p: p follows from q.
>
> **5.122**   If p follows from q, the sense of "p" is extracted from the sense of "q".
>
> **5.123**   If God creates a world in which certain sentences are true, then God thereby creates a world in which all the sentences that follow

from them are true. Similarly, God could not create a world in which sentence "p" were true without creating all the objects designated by it.

5.124 A sentence affirms every sentence that follows from it.

5.1241 "$p.q$" is one of the sentences that affirms "p" while also affirming one of the sentences that affirms "q".

Two sentences oppose each other when no meaningful sentence[90] affirms them both.

5.13 Whether the truth of one sentence follows from the truth of other sentences can be seen in the structure of the sentences.

5.131 That the truth of one sentence follows from the truth of others is expressed by relations in which the forms of those sentences stand to one another: nor need we set up these relations between them by combining them with one another into a single sentence. These relations are internal and exist simultaneously with, and through, the existence of the sentences.

5.1311 When from p v q and ~p we infer q, the relation between the forms of the sentences "p v q" and "~p" is concealed by our method of symbolizing. But if instead of "p v q" we write "$p|q.|.p|q$" and instead of "~p" we write "$p|p$", (where $p|q$ = neither p nor q),[91] then the inner connection [the inference from $(p|q.|.p|q)$ and $(p|p)$ to $(q|q.|.q|q)$] becomes apparent.

(The possibility of inference from $(x).fx$ to fa shows us that the symbol $(x).fx$ has itself generality already in it.)

5.132 If p follows from q, I can make an inference from q to p, deduce p from q.

The manner of inference can only be drawn from the two sentences.

Only they alone can offer any possible justification for the inference.

"Laws of inference," which—as in Frege and Russell—supposedly justify inferences, are senseless and completely superfluous.

5.133 All inference takes place a priori.

5.134 From an elementary sentence no other can be inferred.

5.135 There is no possible way to make an inference from the existence of one fact to the existence of another, entirely different, fact.

5.136 There is no causal linkage to justify any such inference.

5.1361 The future *cannot* be inferred from the present.

Superstition is the belief in causal "linkage."

5.1362 Free will consists in the impossibility of our knowing future actions now. Future actions could only be known if causality were a form of logical inference and had some such *inner* necessity. The connection between knowledge and the known is that of logical necessity.

("A knows that p is the case" makes no sense if p is a tautology.)

5.1363   If the truth of a sentence does not *follow* from the fact of its seeming obvious to us, then obviousness in no way justifies our belief in its truth.

5.14   If a sentence follows from another, then the latter says more than the former and the former says less than the latter.

5.141   If p follows from q and q follows from p, then they are one and the same sentence.[92]

5.142   A tautology follows from all propositions: it says nothing.

5.143   A contradiction is that which is common to sentences that *no* sentence has in common with any other. A tautology is that which is common to all sentences that have nothing in common with each other.

Contradiction vanishes, so to speak, outside, and tautology inside, all sentences.

Contradiction is the outer boundary of sentences; tautology is the insubstantial point at their center.

5.15   If T_r is the number of truth-grounds of sentence "r", T_{rs} the number of truth-grounds of sentence "s" that are at the same time truth-grounds of "r", then let us call the ratio $T_{rs}:T_r$ the measure of the *probability* given by sentence "r" to sentence "s".

5.151   In a schema like the one in 5.101, let T_r be the number of "T's" in sentence r, and let T_{rs} be the number of "T's" in sentence s that stand in those columns where sentence r has "T's". Then sentence r gives to sentence s the probability $T_{rs}:T_r$.

5.1511   There is no separate object unique to probability sentences.

5.152   Sentences that have no truth-arguments in common with each other we call independent.

Two elementary sentences give each other the probability $1/2$.

If p follows from q, then sentence "q" gives sentence "p" the probability 1. The certainty of the logical conclusion is a limiting case of probability.

(Application to tautology and contradiction.)

5.153   A sentence is in itself neither probable nor improbable. An event occurs or does not occur, there is no middle course.

5.154   An urn contains an equal number of black balls and white balls. I draw one ball after another and put them back in the urn. Then I can determine by the experiment that the number of black balls drawn and the number of white balls drawn approximate each other as the drawing continues.[93]

So *this* is not a mathematical truth.

If then I say, "It's equally probable that I will draw a white and a black ball," this means, "all the circumstances known to me (including the laws of nature that I assume by hypothesis to be true) give to the occurrence of the one event no *more* probability than to the occurrence of the other. That is, they give—as can easily be seen from the above explanations—to each event the probability $1/2$.

What I can verify by the experiment is that the occurrence of the two events is independent of the circumstances about which I have only schematic knowledge.

5.155 The unit for a probability statement is: the circumstances—which I only know in part—give a certain degree of probability to the occurrence of a particular event.

5.156 Thus probability is a generalization.

It involves a general description of the form of a sentence.

We use probability in place of certainty—our knowledge of a fact may be incomplete, but at least we know *something* about its form.

(A sentence may be an incomplete picture of a certain fact, but it is always *a* complete picture.)

A probability sentence is, as it were, an extract from other sentences.

5.2 The structures of sentences stand to one another in internal relations.

5.21 We can emphasize these internal relations in our form of expression, by representing one sentence as the result of an operation that produces it out of other sentences (the bases of the operation).

5.22 The operation is the expression of a relation between the structures of its result and of its bases.

5.23 The operation is what has to happen to a sentence to turn it into another one.

5.231 Naturally, that will depend on their formal properties, the internal similarity of their forms.

5.232 A series is ordered by an internal relation equivalent to that of generating one term from another.

5.233 There can be no other than truth-functional operations.

5.234 The truth-functions of the elementary sentences are the results of operations with the elementary sentences as bases. (These operations I call truth-operations).

5.2341 The sense of a truth-function of p is a function of the sense of p.

Negation, logical addition, logical multiplication, etc., etc., are operations.

(Negation reverses the sense of sentences.)

5.24 An operation shows itself in a variable; it shows how we can get from one sentence form to another.

It expresses the difference between the forms.

(And the bases themselves are what the bases of an operation and the result have in common.)

5.241 An operation does not characterize a form but only the difference between forms.

5.242 The same operation that produces "q" from "p" produces "r" from "q", and so on. There is but one way of expressing this: "p", "q", "*r*", etc., are variables that give general expression to certain formal relations.

5.25   The occurrence of an operation does not characterize the sense of a sentence.

For the operation does not assert anything, only its result does, and this depends on the bases of the operation.

(Operation and function must not be confused with one another.)

5.251   A function cannot be its own argument, but the result of an operation can be the base of that very operation.

5.252   This is the only possible way of stepping from one term of a formal series to a term in another formal series (from type to type in the hierarchies of Russell and Whitehead). (Russell and Whitehead did not allow such steps but took them repeatedly themselves.)

5.2521   When an operation is repeatedly applied to its own results, I call it a *successive application.* (Thus, "$O'O'O'a$" is the end result of three successive applications of the operation "$O'\xi$" to "a".)

Similarly, I speak of the successive application of *multiple* operations to a number of sentences.

5.2522   For the general term of the formal series $a, O'a, O'O'a, \ldots$ I use the sign "$[a, x, O'x]$". The bracketed expression is a variable. The first term marks the beginning of the formal series, the second is the form of a term x selected arbitrarily from the formal series, and the third is the formal term immediately following x in the series.

5.2523   The concept of the successive application of an operation is equivalent to the concept "and so on."

5.253   One operation can reverse the effect of another. Operations can cancel each other out.

5.254   Operations can vanish (e.g., negation in "$\sim\sim p$"$\cdot$"$\sim\sim p = p$").

5.3   All sentences are the result of truth-operations on the elementary sentences.

The truth operation is the way in which a truth-function arises from elementary sentences.

According to the nature of truth-operations, truth-functions generate further truth functions in the same way that elementary sentences generate their own truth-functions. Every truth-operation creates from truth-functions of elementary sentences another truth-function of elementary sentences, that is, another sentence. The result of every truth-operation on the results of truth-operations on elementary sentences is also the result of one truth-operation on elementary sentences.

Every sentence is the result of truth-operations on elementary sentences.

5.31   The schemata in 4.31 are also meaningful even when "p","q", "r", etc., are not elementary sentences.

And one can easily see that the sentence in 4.442 expresses a single truth-function of elementary sentences even when "p" and "q" are truth functions of elementary sentences.

5.32 All truth-functions are results of successive applications of a finite number of truth-operations to elementary sentences.

5.4 It is here that the nonexistence of "logical objects" or "logical constants" (in the sense of Frege and Russell) shows itself.

5.41 For: all results of truth-operations on truth-functions are always identical whenever they are one and the same truth function of elementary sentences.

5.42 That v, ⊃, etc., are not relations in the sense of right and left, etc., is obvious.

The possibility of defining crosswise the primitive signs of Frege and Russell shows by itself that they are not primitive nor do they signify any relations.

And it is obvious that the "⊃" that we define by means of "~" and "v" is identical with that by which we define "v" with the help of "~", and that this second "v" is identical with the first, and so on.

5.43 That from a fact *p* infinitely many *others* should follow, namely, ~~*p*, ~~~~*p*, etc., seems impossible. And it seems even stranger that the infinite number of sentences of logic (mathematics) follow from half a dozen "primitive sentences."[94]

Actually, all the sentences of logic say the same thing. Namely, nothing.

5.44 Truth-functions are not material functions.

If, for an example, a double negation is an affirmation, is the negation—in any sense—contained in the affirmation? Does "~~*p*" negate ~*p*, or does it affirm *p*, or both?

In no sense is the sentence "~~*p*" about negation, for negation is not an object; on the other hand, the possibility of negation is already presupposed in affirmation.

And if there were an object called "~", then "~~p" would have to say something different from what "*p*" says, since in that case the one sentence would be about ~ and the other would not.

5.441 The disappearance of apparent logical constants happens also in "~(∃x).~*f*x", which is equivalent to "(x).*f*x", and in "(∃x).*f*x.x=*a*", which is equivalent to "*f*a".

5.442 When a sentence is given us, so is given *with it* the results of all truth-operations that have it as their basis.

5.45 If logical primitive signs, then any correct logic must clearly show their relative status and justify their presence [*Dasein*]. The construction of logic *out of* its primitive signs must be clearly shown.

5.451 If logic has primitive ideas,[95] these must be independent of one another. If a primitive idea is introduced, it must be introduced for all the contexts in which it occurs at all. One cannot therefore introduce it first for *one* context and then again for another. For instance, once negation is introduced it must be clearly understandable both in sentences of the form "~*p*" and in sentences like "~*p* v q)",

"$(\exists x).{\sim}fx$", etc. We cannot introduce it first for one class of cases and then all over again for the other, for then it would be very doubtful whether the term meant the same in both cases, and there would be no ground for using the same kind of connective in both cases.

(In short, what Frege said [in *The Fundamental Laws of Arithmetic*] about the introduction of signs by means of definitions holds, *mutatis mutandis,* for the introduction of primitive signs.[96])

5.452   The introduction of any new device into the symbolism must always be a momentous event. No new symbol may be "innocently" introduced in logic using brackets or in a footnote with a perfectly innocent face.

(Thus in *Principia Mathematica* Russell and Whitehead suddenly present a definition and a fundamental law in words. Why the sudden appearance of words? It requires justification but of course they don't give any because they can't, the whole procedure is forbidden.)

But if at some point there is a need for a new symbol, we must first ask: when will the use of this device now become unavoidable? Its proper place in logic must be clearly shown.

5.453   All use of numbers in logic requires justification.

Or, on the contrary: it must be cleared up that there are no numbers in logic.

There are no privileged numbers.

5.454   In logic there is no side-by-side and no classification can be given.

In logic no distinction can be made between the general and the specific.

5.4541   The solutions to logical problems should be simple, since they set the standard of simplicity.

People have always quietly accepted the idea that there must be a realm in which answers to all questions fit perfectly together—a priori—into a closed, regular structure.

A domain ruled by one law: "Simplicity is the hallmark of truth."[97]

5.46   When we have properly introduced the logical signs, we have introduced the sense of all their combinations at the same time; that is, not only "pvq" but "$\sim$(pv$\sim$q)" as well, etc., etc. We should then already have introduced the effect of all possible combinations of brackets; and we would thereby have made clear that the proper general primitive signs of logic are not "pvq", "$(\exists x).fx$", etc., but rather the most general form of their combinations.

5.461   The apparently unimportant fact that logical pseudorelations like v and ⊃—unlike real relations—need brackets is significant.

The use of brackets with these apparently indefinable signs indicates that they are not the real indefinable signs of logic. And surely no one could believe that brackets have an independent meaning.

5.4611   The logical operation signs are punctuation-marks.

5.47 Clearly, whatever can be said *from the very* beginning about the form of all sentences, must be sayable *all at once.*

All logical operations can be expressed in terms of the elementary sentences themselves. For "*fa*" says the same thing as

$$(\exists x).fx.x{=}a".$$

Where there is complexity, there is argument and function, and where these are present, there are already all the logical constants.

One could say: the sole logical constant is what *all* sentences, by their nature, have in common.

This however is the general form of a sentence.

5.471 The general form of a sentence is the essence of a sentence.

> **5.4711** The essence of a sentence gives the essence of all description and therefore reveals the essence of the world.[98]

5.472 The description of the most general form of a sentence is itself the description of the one and only general primitive sign in logic.

5.473 Logic must take care of itself.

> If a sign is *possible,* it is capable of signifying something. Everything that is possible in logic is also permitted. ("Socrates is identical" does not mean anything because there is no such quality as "identical." The sentence is nonsensical because we have not made some arbitrary determination but not because of the symbol being impermissible in itself.)
>
> That is the sense in which we cannot make mistakes in logic.

> **5.4731** The self-evidence that Russell talked so much about can be completely dispensed with in logic because language itself absolutely forbids all logical mistakes. What makes logic a priori is the impossibility of thinking illogically.

> **5.4732** We cannot give the wrong sense to a sign.

>> **5.47321** Naturally, Occam's razor is no arbitrary rule, nor one that is merely justified by successful application: its message is that *unnecessary* signs in a symbolic language are meaningless, they refer to nothing.

> **5.4733** Frege says: any well-formed sentence must have a sense; and I say: every possible sentence is well-formed, and if it doesn't make sense, that can only be because we have failed to give any reference for some of its constituents.
>
> (Even if we think we have.)
>
> Thus, "Socrates is identical" says nothing, because we have given *no adjectival* meaning to the word "identical." For when it appears as a sign for identity, it symbolizes in an entirely different way—the signifying relation is different—therefore the symbol is in the two cases entirely different; the two symbols have the sign in common with one another only by accident.

5.474 The number of fundamental operations we need depends *solely* on our notation.

5.475 We need only construct a system of signs with the right number of dimensions—with a fitting mathematical variety.

5.476 Clearly, then, the question is not how many fundamental ideas have to be given expression, but rather how to express a rule.[99]

5.5 Each truth-function is a result of successive applications of the operation

$$\text{``(-----T)}(\xi,....)\text{''}.$$

This operation negates all the sentences in the right-hand brackets and so I call it the negation of those sentences.

5.501 When the terms of a bracketed expression are sentences—and their order inside the brackets is irrelevant—I indicate this by a sign of the form "$(\bar{\xi})$". "ξ" is a variable whose values are terms of the bracketed expression and the bar over it signifies that it is the representative of all the values inside the brackets.

(E.g., if ξ has three values, P, Q, and R, then
$$(\bar{\xi}) = (P,Q,R).)$$

The values of the variable are prescribed.

The prescription is a description of the sentences having the variable as their representative.

We can distinguish three types of description: 1. Direct enumeration. In this case we substitute for the variable the constants that are its values. 2. Giving a function fx whose values for all values of x are the sentences that are to be described. 3. Giving a formal law, according to which those sentences are constructed, in which case the bracketed expression has as its members all the terms of a formal series.

5.502 Instead of "$(-----T)(\xi,....)$", I can thus write "$N(\bar{\xi})$".

"$N(\bar{\xi})$" is the negation of all the values of the sentence variable ξ.

5.503 It is obviously easy to express using this operation how sentences may and may not be constructed. So it must be possible to express this exactly.

5.51 If ξ has but one value, then $N(\bar{\xi}) = \sim p$ (not p); if it has two values, then $N(\bar{\xi}) = \sim p.\sim q$ (neither p nor q).

5.511 How can the all-embracing logic that mirrors the world rely on so many special hooks and manipulations? Only because all these devices are all connected into an infinitely fine network, the great mirror.

5.512 "$\sim p$" is true when "p" is false. Therefore, in the sentence "$\sim p$", when true, "p" is false. How then can the stroke "$\sim$" make it agree with reality?

Here's how: in "$\sim p$" it is not the "$\sim$" that negates but, rather, the negating is done by what all the signs of this notation have in common.

That is, the common rule governing the construction of "$\sim p$", "$\sim\sim\sim p$", "$\sim p$ v $\sim p$", "$\sim p.\sim p$", etc., etc., ad infinitum, is the common factor that mirrors the negation.

5.513 It could be said that what is common to all symbols that assert p as well as q, is the sentence "$p.q$", and that what is common to all symbols that affirm either p or q is the proposition "p v q".

And in this way we can say: two sentences are opposed to one another, if they have nothing in common and: every sentence has only one negative, because there is only one sentence that lies entirely outside it.

In Russell's notation, too, it appears evident that "$q.p$ v $\sim p$" is equivalent to "q", that "p v $\sim p$" says nothing.

5.514 If a notation is established, there is in it a rule that governs how all the sentences that negate p are constructed, a rule that governs the construction of all sentences that affirm p, a rule that governs the construction of all sentences that affirm p or q, and so on. These rules are equivalent to the symbols and in them their sense is mirrored.

5.515 It must be shown in our symbols that only sentences can be combined with each other by "v", "." [and], etc.

And this is indeed so, for the symbol p in p v q itself presupposes "v", "$\sim$", etc. If the sign "p" in "p v q" does not stand for a complex sign, then by itself it cannot make sense. But then the signs "p v p", "$p.p$", etc., whose sense must be the same as p's, must also not make sense. But if "p v p" does not make sense, then "p v q" cannot make sense either.

5.5151 Does the sign of a negative sentence have to be constructed by means of the sign of the positive? Couldn't we use a negative fact to express a negative sentence? (Like: if "a" does not stand in a certain relation to "b", then we could rely on this fact to express that aRb is not the case.)

Yet even in such a case the negative sentence is constructed by our relying indirectly on the positive.

The positive *sentence* necessarily presupposes the existence of the negative *sentence* and *vice versa*.

5.52 Suppose the value of ξ are all the values of a given function fx for all values of x, then $N(\bar{\xi}) = \sim(\exists x).fx$.

5.521 I separate the concept *all* from the truth-function.

Frege and Russell introduced generality together with logical product or logical sum. This made the sentences "$(\exists x).fx$" and "$(x).fx$", which involve both concepts, difficult to understand.

5.522 What is most peculiar about the generality sign is that it indicates a logical archetype and, second, that it draws attention to constants.

5.523 The sign for generality appears as an argument.

5.524 Once objects are given, that itself gives us *all* objects.

Once elementary sentences are given, that in itself is enough for *all* elementary sentences to be given.

5.525 It is wrong to render the sentence "$(\exists x).fx$" in the words, "fx is *possible*," as Russell does. [100]

Certainty, possibility or impossibility of a fact are expressed, not by a sentence, but by an expression's being a tautology, a meaningful sentence, or a contradiction.

The precedent to which one would always like to appeal must reside in the symbol itself.

5.526   The world can be completely described using fully generalized sentences, that is, without first correlating any name with a particular object.

Then, to arrive at the ordinary mode of expression, we simply need to add, after sentences like "There is an x and there are not an x and a y, such that . . . ," the words "and this x is a."

5.5261   A fully generalized sentence is composite just as every other sentence is. (This shows itself in that "$(\exists x,\phi).(\phi x)$" mentions "$\phi$" and "$x$" separately. Both signs independently stand in a signifying relation to the world, as in ungeneralized sentences.)

A characteristic of a composite symbol: it has something in common with *other* symbols.

5.5262   The truth or falsehood of *every* sentence alters something about the general structure of the world. And the play that is allowed to its structure by the totality of elementary sentences is just that which is limited by the completely general statements.

(If an elementary sentence is true, then, at any rate, there is *one more* elementary sentence that is true.)

5.53   Identity of the object I express by identity of the sign and not by means of a sign of identity. Difference of the objects I express by difference of the signs.

5.5301   That identity is not a relation between objects is obvious. This becomes very clear if, for example, one considers the sentence "$(x):fx.\supset.x=a$". This sentences says simply that *only a* satisfies function f, not that only objects having a certain relation to a satisfy function f.

One might then say that *only a* has this relation to a, but this would have to be expressed using the identity sign.

5.5302   Russell's definition of "$=$" is unsatisfactory, because according to it we cannot assert of two objects that all their properties are in common. (Even if this sentence is never right, it still makes sense.)

5.5303   Roughly put: to assert that *two* objects are identical is nonsense, whereas to assert that *one* thing is identical with itself says nothing.

5.531   I also don't write "$f(a,b).a=b$" but "$f(a,a)$" (or, "$f(b,b)$"). And it's not "$f(a,b).\sim a=b$", but "$f(a,b)$". Likewise, I do not write "$(\exists x,y).f(x,y).x=y$", but, rather, "$(\exists x).f(x,x)$"; and it's not "$(\exists x,y).f(x,y).\sim x=y$", but "$(\exists x.y).f(x,y)$".

5.532   And analogously: not "$(\exists x,y).f(x,y).x=y$" but "$(\exists x).f(x,x)$"; and not "$(\exists x,y).f(x,y).\sim x=y$" but "$(\exists x,y).f(x,y)$."

(Thus Russell's "$(\exists x,y).fxyxy$" becomes "$(\exists x,y).f(x,y).v.(\exists x).f(x,x)$".)

5.5321   Thus "$(x):f(x)\supset x=a$" can be written, for instance, "$(\exists x).f(x).\supset.fa:\sim(\exists x,y).fx.fy$".

And the sentence "*Only one x satisfies* $f(\ )$" will be: "$(\exists x).fx:\sim(\exists x,y).fx.fy$".

5.533   Therefore, the identity sign is not an essential part of logical notation.

5.534   And now we see that pseudosentences[101] such as "*a*=*a*", "*a*=*b*. *b*=*c*.⊃*a*=*c*", "(*x*).*x*=*x*", "(∃*x*).*x*=*a*", etc., cannot even be written down using correct conceptual notation.

5.535   This clears up all the problems having to do with such pseudo-sentences.

The resolution of all problems having to do with Russell's "axiom of infinity" can now be given.

What the Axiom of Infinity is supposed to show would be expressed in language by there being infinitely many names with different meanings.

> **5.5351**   In some cases it may be tempting to use expressions of the form "*a*=*a*" or "*p*⊃*p*" and other such expressions. This is exactly what happens when one wants to say something about the archetype Sentence, Thing, etc. So Russell in his *Principles of Mathematics* renders nonsense such as "*p* is a sentence" symbolically as "*p*⊃*p*", and then places it in front of sentences as an antecedent hypothesis so as to show that their places for arguments can only be occupied by sentences.
>
> (It is meaningless to use "*p*⊃*p*" as an antecedent to ensure that the arguments of the consequent will have the right form. First, with a non-sentence as argument, the antecedent becomes not merely false but meaningless; second, using the wrong sort of arguments makes the sentence itself meaningless. So in this way it saves itself from the wrong arguments just as well, or as badly, as the meaningless antecedent that was supposed to have done this in the first place.)
>
> **5.5352**   Similarly, some have tried to express the thought "There are no things" by writing "~(∃*x*).*x*=*x*". If this were actually a sentence, wouldn't the sentence be just as true if "there *were* things" but such that no thing was identical with itself?[102]

5.54   In their general form, sentences occur in other sentences only as bases of truth-operations.

> **5.541**   At first glance, it appears as if there were another way in which one sentence could occur in another.
>
> Especially in certain forms of sentences in psychology, such as "A believes that p is the case" or "A thinks p," etc.
>
> Here it appears superficially as if the sentence p stood in some sort of relation to an object A.
>
> (And these sentences have actually been so taken in modern theory of knowledge [Russell, Moore, etc.].)
>
> **5.542**   Clearly, however, "A believes that *p*," "A thinks *p*," "A says *p*," are of the form "'*p*' says *p*", and this in no way involves a correlation of fact to object, but rather the correlation of facts by means of the correlation of their objects.

5.5421 This also shows that the soul—the subject, etc.—as conceived in contemporary superficial psychology, does not exist.

For a composite soul would no longer be a soul.

5.5422 The correct explanation of the form of the sentence "A judges that p" must show the impossibility of a judgment being a piece of nonsense. (Russell's theory does not satisfy this condition.)

5.5423 Perceiving a complex means perceiving the way its components are related.

This also explains the sort of phenomena illustrated by the following figure, which can be seen as a cube in two different ways:

For we really see two different facts.

(If I look first at the corners marked *a* and only glance at the *b*'s, the *a*'s appear in front and vice versa.)

5.55 The question about all the possible forms of elementary sentences must now be answered a priori.

Elementary sentences consist of names. However, since we cannot specify the number of names having different meanings, we cannot give the composition of elementary sentences.

5.551 One fundamental principle is this: whenever we can answer a question using logic we must be able to answer it without a lot of fuss.

(And if we ever have to look at the world for the answer to such a question, this shows us that we have gone off on a completely wrong track.)

5.552 The "experience" we need to understand logic is not that soandso is the case, but simply that it *is:* that, however, is not an experience.

Logic precedes every experience—that something is soandso.

It is before the How, not before the What.

5.5521 If this were not the case, how could we apply logic? Let me put it this way: since even if there were no world there would still be logic, how could it possibly be the case that there be logic given that there is a world?

5.553 Russell said that there were simple relations between different numbers of things (individuals). But between what numbers? And how is this to be decided? By experience?

(There is no privileged number.)

5.554 To enumerate any specific forms would be entirely arbitrary.

5.5541 Russell supposes it is possible to answer a priori the question whether I can get into a situation in which I need the sign for a relation having 27 terms to signify something.

5.5542   But can it even be legitimate to ask such a question? How can we set up a form of a sign unless we first know that it is possible that something corresponds to it?

Does it make any sense to ask what must there *be* such that something can be the case?

5.555   It is clear that we have a concept of elementary sentences independently of their particular logical forms.

But when we have a system for creating symbols, what is most important for logic is the system itself, not the individual symbols it produces.

And in any case, how could logic demand that I must deal with forms that I can invent? Logic demands that I must deal with that which makes it possible for me to invent forms.

5.556   There can be no hierarchy of forms of elementary sentences. We can only foresee what we ourselves can construct.

5.5561   Empirical reality is bounded by the totality of objects. This boundary reveals itself throughout the totality of elementary sentences.

The hierarchies are and must be independent of reality.

5.5562   If we know on purely logical grounds that there must be elementary sentences, this must be known by anyone who understands sentences in their unanalyzed form.

5.5563   All the sentences of ordinary language are actually, just as they are, logically and completely in order. The completely simple thing that we must here formulate is not a mere likeness of the truth but the truth in its totality.

(Our problems are not abstract but, on the contrary, about as concrete as you can get.)

5.557   The *application* of logic is what decides what elementary sentences there are.

Logic cannot foresee in advance what belongs to its application.

Clearly, logic must never collide with its application.

But logic must always remain in touch with its application.

Therefore, logic and its application must not overlap each other.

5.5571   Since I cannot make a list of elementary sentences a priori, any attempt to make such a list must lead to nonsense.

5.6   *The boundary of my language* is the boundary of my world.

5.61   Logic fills the world: the boundary of logic is also the boundary of the world.

So in logic we cannot say "The world has this in it and this, but not that."

For that would apparently presuppose that some possibilities were thereby being excluded, which cannot possibly be the case, since this would require that logic should extend beyond the boundary of the world; for only then could it have a view from the other side of the boundary.

What we cannot think, that we cannot think: we cannot therefore *say* what we cannot think.

5.62   This thought itself shows how much truth there is in solipsism.

What the solipsist intends to say is absolutely correct. The problem is that the truth cannot speak but only shows itself.

That the world is my world reveals itself in the fact that the boundary of language (the language that I alone understand) is the boundary of my world.

5.621   The world and life are one. [103]

5.63   I am my world. (The microcosm.)

5.631   The thinking, perceiving subject does not exist.

If I were to write a book, *The World as I Found It,* I would also have to include an account of my body in it, and report which parts are subject to my will and which are not, etc. This then would be a method of isolating the subject, or rather of showing that in an important sense there is no subject; that is to say, of it alone in this book mention could *not* be made.

5.632   The subject does not belong to the world but is the boundary of the world.

5.633   Where *in* the world could a metaphysical subject be?

You say this is just like the case with the eye and the visual field. But you do *not* really see the eye.

And there is nothing *in the visual field* to let you infer that it is being seen through an eye.

5.6331   For the form of the visual is clearly not like this:

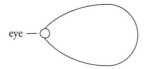

5.634   This is connected with the fact that no aspect of our experience is a priori.

Everything we see could be other than it is.

Everything we describe could be other than it is.

There is no arrangement of things a priori.

5.64   Here we can see that solipsism [104] thoroughly thought out coincides with pure realism. The *I* in solipsism shrinks to an extensionless point and there remains the reality coordinated with it.

5.641   Thus there really is a sense in which philosophy can speak about the self in a nonpsychological way.

The *I* occurs in philosophy through the fact that the "world is my world."

The philosophical *I* is not the human being, not the human body, nor the human soul with which psychology deals. The philosophical self is the metaphysical subject, the boundary—nowhere in the world.

6   The general form of a truth-function is $[p,\bar{\xi},N(\bar{\xi})]$.

This is the general form of a sentence.

6.001   This says only that every sentence is the result of successive applications of the operation $N'(\bar{\xi})$ to the elementary sentences.

6.002   If we are given the general form of the way in which a sentence is constructed, then we are thereby also given the general form of the way in which by an operation out of one sentence we can create another.

6.01   The general form of the operation $\Omega'(\bar{n})$ is therefore:

$$[\bar{\xi}, N(\bar{\xi})]'(\bar{n})\ (=[\bar{n}, \bar{\xi}\ N(\bar{\xi})]).$$

This is the most general form of transition from one sentence to another.

6.02   And thus we come to numbers: I define

$$x = \Omega^{0,}x \text{ Def. and}$$
$$\Omega'\Omega^{y,}x = \Omega^{y+1,}x \text{ Def.}$$

According, then, to these symbolic rules
write the series $x,\ \Omega'x,\ \Omega'\Omega'x,\ \Omega'\Omega'\Omega'x\ldots$
as: $\Omega^{0,}x,\ \Omega^{0+1,}x,\ \Omega^{0+1+1,}x,\ \Omega^{0+1+1+1,}x\ldots$
Therefore I write in place of "$[x, \xi, \Omega'\ \xi]$",
"$[\Omega^{0,}x,\ \Omega^{y,}x,\ \Omega^{y+1,}x]$".
And I define:
0+1=1 Def.
0+1+1=2 Def.
0+1+1+1=3 Def.
and so on.

6.021   A number is the exponent of an operation.

6.022   The concept "number" is simply what is common to all numbers, the general form of a number.

The concept "number" is the variable number.

And the concept of numerical equality is the general form of all particular cases of numerical equality.

6.03   The general form for integers is $[0,\xi,\xi+1]$.

6.031   The theory of classes is altogether superfluous in mathematics.

This is connected with the fact that the generality that we need in mathematics is not an *accidental* one.

6.1   The sentences of logic are tautologies.

6.11   The sentences of logic therefore say nothing. (They are analytic sentences.)

6.111 Theories that make a sentence of logic appear to have real content are always false. It might be thought, for example, that the words "true" and "false" denote two properties among other properties, and then it would look like a remarkable fact that every sentence possesses one of these properties. This now seems no more obvious than the sentence "All roses are either red or yellow" would seem, even if it were true. Indeed, the logical sentence acquires all the characteristics of a sentence of natural science, and this is a sure sign that it has been wrongly construed.

6.112 The correct explanation of logical sentences must give them a peculiar position among all sentences.

6.113 It is the characteristic mark of logical sentences that one can perceive in the symbol alone that they are true; and this fact contains in itself the whole philosophy of logic. And so also it is one of the most important facts that the truth or falsehood of nonlogical sentences can *not* be recognized from the sentences alone.

6.12 The fact that the sentences of logic are tautologies shows the formal—logical—properties of language, of the world.

That its constituent parts connected together *in this way* form a tautology is a characteristic of its constituent parts.

To be able to form a tautology, sentences connected together in a definite way must have definite properties of structure. That they form a tautology when *so* connected shows therefore that they possess these properties of structure.

6.1201 That for example the sentences "p" and "$\sim p$" in the conjunction "$\sim(p.\sim p)$" form a tautology shows that they contradict each other. That the sentences "$p \supset q$" "p", and "q" conjoined into "$(p \supset q) . (p) : \supset : q$" form a tautology shows that q follows from p and $p \supset q$. That "$(x),fx. \supset :fa$" forms a tautology shows that fa follows from $(x).fx.$ etc., etc.

6.1202 Clearly, we could have used for this purpose contradictions instead of tautologies.

6.1203 To recognize a tautology as such, we can, in cases in which no sign of generality occurs in the tautology, make use of the following intuitive method: I write instead of "p", "q", "r", etc., "TpF", "TqF", "TrF", etc. The truth-combinations I express by brackets, for example:

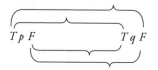

and the coordination of the truth or falsity of the whole sentence with the truth-combinations of the truth-arguments by lines in the following way:

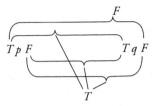

This sign, for example, would therefore present the sentence
$p \supset q$. Now I will proceed to inquire whether a sentence such as
$\sim(p. \sim p)$ (The Law of Contradiction) is a tautology. The form
"$\sim\xi$" is written in our notation

the form "$\xi.\eta$" thus:

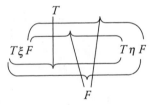

Hence the sentence $\sim(p. \sim q)$ runs thus:

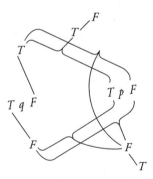

If here we put "p" instead of "q" and examine the combination
of the outermost T and F with the innermost, it is seen that the
truth of the whole sentence is coordinated with *all* the truth-
combinations of its argument, its falsity with none of the truth-
combinations.

6.121 The sentences of logic demonstrate the logical properties of sentences, by combining them into sentences that say nothing.

This could be called a zero-method. Sentences are brought into equilibrium in a logical sentence, and then this state of equilibrium shows how these sentences must be logically constructed.

6.122 This shows that we can carry on without logical sentences, since in proper notation we can recognize the formal properties of the sentences merely by inspecting them.

6.1221 If, for example, two sentences "p" and "q" form a tautology, then clearly q follows from p.

For instance, that "q" follows from "$p \supset .q.p$" can be seen from these two sentences themselves, but we can also show it by combining them into "$p \supset q.p: \supset :q$" and then showing that this is a tautology.

6.1222 This throws light on the question of why logical sentences can no more be confirmed empirically than they can be refuted empirically. Not only must a sentence of logic be incapable of being contradicted by any possible experience, it must likewise be incapable of being confirmed by experience.

6.1223 It becomes clear now why we often feel as though "logical truths" must be "*postulated*" by us. Actually, we can postulate them insofar as we can postulate a proper notation.

6.1224 It now also becomes clear why logic was thought of as the theory of forms and of inference.

6.123 Clearly, the laws of logic cannot themselves obey further logical laws.

(Russell was wrong in supposing that there is a special law of contradiction for every "type"; one law is sufficient, since it is not applied to itself.)

6.1231 General validity is *not* the mark of logical sentences.

For to be general only means to be accidentally valid for all objects. An ungeneralized sentence can be a tautology just as well as a generalized one.

6.1232 General logical validity could be called essential rather than the accidental general validity of sentences like "All people are mortal." Sentences like Russell's "axiom of reducibility" are not logical sentences, which explains our feeling that, if true, they can only be true by lucky coincidence.

6.1233 We can conceive a world in which the axiom of reducibility is invalid. But clearly, logic has nothing to do with the question of whether our world is really like that or not.

6.124 The sentences of logic describe the scaffolding of the world, or rather, they present it. They are not *about* anything. They presuppose that names mean something, that elementary sentences make sense [express thoughts]: and that is their connection to the world. Clearly, that some combinations of essentially determinate symbols are tautologies says something about the world. That's the decisive point.

We said that in the symbols that we use, there is something arbitrary, something not. In logic only the latter expresses; but this means that in logic it is not *we* who express, by means of signs, what we want; in logic the nature of inevitably necessary signs *speaks for itself.* Thus in learning the logical syntax of any symbolic language we are *given* all the sentences of logic.

6.125 It is possible, even with the old conception of logic, to give from the start a description of all "true" logical sentences.

6.1251 Hence there can *never* be surprises in logic.

6.126 By calculating the logical properties of the *symbol,* we can calculate whether a sentence belongs to logic.

And that's what we do when we "prove" a sentence in logic. For without bother about sense and meaning, we form the logical sentences out of others by mere *symbolic rules.*

Here is how we prove a sentence in logic: we create it out of other sentences by successively applying certain operations that again generate tautologies out of the first. (Only a tautology can *follow* from a tautology.)

6.1261 In logic, process and result are equivalent. (Hence, no surprises.)

6.1262 Proof in logic is nothing but a mechanical procedure for facilitating the recognition of it as a tautology.

6.1263 Indeed, it would be an incredible coincidence if a meaningful sentence could be proved *logically* from others, just as a sentence in logic can. Clearly, proving logically that some meaningful sentence is true is completely different from a proof in logic.

6.1264 The meaningful sentence asserts something, and its proof shows that it is so; in logic every sentence is the form of a proof.

Every sentence in logic is a symbolic presentation of a *modus ponens.* (And the *modus ponens* cannot be expressed by a sentence.)

6.1265 Logic can always be conceived in such a way that every sentence is its own proof.

6.127 All sentences in logic are of equal rank, rather than some being essentially primitive from which the others are derived.

Every tautology shows itself that it is a tautology.

6.1271 Clearly, the number of "primitive sentences of logic" is arbitrary, since we could deduce logic from one primitive sentence simply by forming, for example, the logical product of Frege's primitive sentences. (Frege might say that this would no longer be immediately self-evident. But what is amazing is that a thinker as precise as Frege nevertheless appealed to the degree of self-evidence as his criterion of what a logical sentence is.)

6.13 Logic is not a theory about the world but a reflection of it, its mirror image.

Logic is transcendent. [105]

6.2 Mathematics is a logical method.

Mathematical sentences are equations and, therefore, pseudo-statements.[106]

6.21 Mathematical sentences express no thoughts.

6.211 In our daily lives we never need mathematical sentences, we use them only to infer from sentences that are not a part of mathematics to other sentences that also are not mathematical.

(In philosophy the question "Why do we really use that word, that sentence?" always leads to valuable insights.)

6.22 The logic of the world that the sentences of logic show to be tautologies, mathematics shows to be equations.

6.23 If two expressions are connected by the sign of equality, this means that they can be substituted for one another. But whether this is the case must be visible in the two expressions themselves.

That two expressions can be substituted for one another characterizes their logical form.

6.231 A property of affirmation is that it can be conceived as double denial.

A property of "1+1+1+1" is that it can be conceived as "(1+1)+(1+1)".

6.232 According to Frege, all these expressions have the same meaning but different senses.

But what is essential about an equation is that it is not necessary to show that both expressions, which are connected by the sign of equality, have the same meaning: this can be seen from the two expressions themselves.

6.2321 And that the sentences of mathematics can be proved means nothing more than this: their correctness can be seen without our having to compare the sentences, what they express, with the facts, in terms of correctness.

6.2322 The identity of the meaning of two expressions cannot be *asserted*. To be able to assert anything about their meaning, I must first know their meaning, and if I already know their meaning, I then know whether they mean the same or something else.

6.2323 The equation merely characterizes the point of view from which I consider the two expressions, that is, from the point of view of their equality of meaning.

6.233 The question of whether we need intuition for the solution of mathematical problems must be answered in this way: here language itself is the necessary intuition.

6.2331 The process of calculation brings about just this intuition.

Calculation is not an experiment.

6.234 Mathematics is a method of logic.

6.2341 The essence of the mathematical method is working with equations. As a consequence of this method, every sentence in mathematics must be self-evident.

6.24 The way mathematics arrives at its equations is by the method of substitution.

For equations express the substitutability of two expressions, and we proceed from a number of equations to new ones, replacing expressions by others in accordance with the equations.

6.241 Thus the proof of the proposition 2×2=4 runs:

$$(\Omega^v)^{\mu'}x = \Omega^{v\times u\,'}x \text{ Def.}$$
$$\Omega^{2\times 2\,'}x = (\Omega^2)^{2\,'}x = (\Omega^2)^{1+1\,'}x = \Omega^{2\,'}\Omega^{2\,'}x = \Omega^{1+1\,'}\Omega^{1+1\,'}x$$
$$= (\Omega'\Omega)'(\Omega'\Omega)'x = \Omega'\Omega'\Omega'\Omega'x = \Omega^{1+1+1+1\,'}x = \Omega^{4\,'}x.$$

6.3 The investigation of logic means the investigation of *all* conformity to *laws*. And outside logic, all is accident.

6.31 The so-called law of induction cannot in any way be a logical law, for obviously it is a meaningful sentence. And therefore it cannot be an a priori law either.

6.32 The law of causality is not a law but the form of a law. [107]

6.321 "Law of causality" is a general name. And just as in mechanics there are, for instance, minimum-laws, such as that of least action, so in physics there are causal laws, laws of the form of causality.

6.3211 People thought that there must be *a* "law of least action" even before they knew exactly what it was. (Here, as always, a priori certainty turns out to be something purely logical.)

6.33 We do not *believe* a priori in a law of conservation; rather, we *know* a priori the possibility of a logical form.

6.34 All sentences, such as the law of causation, the law of continuity in nature, the law of least expenditure in nature, etc., etc., all these are a priori intuitions of possible forms of sentences in science.

6.341 Newtonian mechanics, for instance, brings the description of the universe into a unified form. Imagine a white surface with irregular black spots. We then say: Whatever kind of picture these make I can always get as near as I like to its description, provided I cover the surface with some sufficiently fine square network and then say of each square that it is either white or black. In this way I bring the description of the surface into a unified form. The form itself is arbitrary because I could have applied with equal success a net with, say, a triangular or hexagonal mesh. It might be that the description would then have been simpler, that is, we might well have described the surface more accurately with a triangular and coarser, rather than with the finer, square mesh, or vice versa, and so on. To such different networks correspond different systems of describing the world. Mechanics determine a form of description by saying that all sentences in the description of the world must be obtained in a given way from a certain number of already given sentences, the mechanical axioms. It thus provides the bricks for building the edifice of science and says: Whatever building you would erect, you must construct it in some manner with these, and only these, bricks.

(Just as within the system of numbers we must be able to write down any arbitrary number, so within the system of mechanics we must be able to write down any arbitrary physical sentence.)

6.342   And now we can see the position of logic in relation to mechanics. (We construct the network out of indifferent kinds of figures, such as triangles and hexagons together.) That such a picture can be described by a network of a given form asserts *nothing* about the picture. (For this holds of every picture of this kind.) But *this* does characterize the picture in that it can be described *completely* by a particular net with a *particular* size mesh.

Likewise, that the world can be described by Newtonian mechanics says nothing about the world, but it does say something, namely, that the world can be described in that particular way. The fact, too, that the world can be described more simply by one system of mechanics rather than by some other says something about the world.

6.343   Mechanics can be seen as an attempt to construct according to a single plan all *true* sentences that we need for the description of the world.

6.3432   Let us not forget that the mechanical description of the world must always be general. There is, for instance, never any mention of *particular* material points in it, but always only of *some points or other.*

6.35   Although the spots in our picture are geometrical figures, geometry can obviously say nothing about their actual form and position. But the network is *purely* geometrical, and all its properties can be given a priori.

Laws, like the law of causation, etc., are of the network and not of what the network describes.

6.36   If there were a law of causality, it might go like this: "There are natural laws."

But clearly, no one can say this: it shows itself.

6.361   In Hertz's terminology we might say: Only *uniform* connections are *thinkable.*

6.3611   We cannot compare any process with the "passage of time"— there is no such thing—but only with another process (say, with the movement of the chronometer).

The description of the temporal sequence of events is thus only possible if we support ourselves on another process.

The same is true of space. When, for instance, we say that neither of two (mutually exclusive) events can occur, because there is *no cause* why one rather than another should occur, it is clearly a matter of our being unable to describe *one* of the two events unless there is some sort of asymmetry. And if there *is* such an asymmetry, we can regard this as the cause of the occurrence of the one and of the nonoccurrence of the other.

6.63111   The Kantian problem of the right and left hands that cannot cover each other already exists in the plane, and already

there even in one-dimensional space where two congruent figures, *a* and *b*, cannot be made to cover each other without

$$- - - \!\!\!\overset{}{\circ}\!\!\!-\!\!\!-\!\!\!\times - - \times\!\!\!-\!\!\!-\!\!\!\overset{}{\circ} - - -$$
$$\quad\quad a \quad\quad\quad\quad\quad\quad\quad b$$

moving them out of this space. The right and left hands are in
fact completely congruent. And the fact that they cannot be
made to cover each other has nothing to do with it.

A right-hand glove could be put on a left hand if it could be
turned around in four-dimensional space.

6.362 What can be described can also happen, and what is excluded by
the law of causality cannot be described.

6.363 The process of induction is the process of assuming the *simplest*
law that can be reconciled with our experience.

6.3631 However, this process has no logical foundation, only a psychological one.

Clearly, there are no reasons for believing that the simplest
course of events will really happen.

6.36311 That the sun will rise tomorrow is a hypothesis, which
means that we do not *know* whether the sun will rise.

6.37 Nothing forces one thing to happen because something else has happened. The only kind of necessity is *logical* necessity.

6.371 The entire modern worldview is based on the illusion that the
so-called laws of nature can explain natural phenomena.

6.372 People thus treat the laws of nature as if they were unassailable,
which is how the ancients treated God and Fate.

And they are right but also wrong, except the ancients were far
clearer, in that they recognized a clear endpoint—whereas the mod-
erns make it seem as if *everything* is explained.

6.373 The world exists independently of my will.

6.374 Even if everything we wished for would happen, this would only
have been granted, so to say, by fate, for there is no *logical* connection
between the will and the world that could guarantee such a thing;
and the assumed physical connection itself is not something we can
will.

6.375 Just as there is only *logical* necessity, so there is only *logical* impossibility.

6.3751 For instance, that two colors could be at one place in the visual
field at the same time is logically impossible, since it is excluded
by the logical structure of color.

Let us look at how this contradiction presents itself in physics.
It goes something like this: That a particle cannot have two different velocities at the same time, i.e., that it cannot be at two different places at the same time, i.e., that particles at different places
at the same time cannot be identical.

(Clearly, the logical product of two elementary sentences can be neither a tautology nor a contradiction. The assertion that a point in the visual field is two different colors at the same time is a contradiction.)

6.4 All sentences are of equal value.

6.41 The meaning of the world must lie outside the world. In the world everything is as it is, everything happens as it does happen; there is no value *in* it—if there were any, the value would be worthless.

For a value to be worth something, it must lie outside all happening and outside being this way or that. For all happening and being this way or that is accidental.

The nonaccidental cannot be found in the world, for otherwise this too would then be accidental.

The value of the world lies outside it.

6.42 Likewise, there can be no sentences in ethics. Sentences cannot express anything higher.

6.421 Clearly, ethics cannot be put into words.

Ethics is transcendent.[108]

(Ethics and esthetics are one.)

6.422 As soon as we set up an ethical law having the form "thou shalt . . . ," our first thought is: So then what if I don't do it? But clearly ethics has nothing to do with punishment and reward in the ordinary sense. The question about the consequences of my action must therefore be irrelevant. At least these consequences will not be events. For there must be something right in that formulation of the question. There must be some sort of ethical reward and ethical punishment, but this must lie in the action itself.

6.423 We cannot speak of the will as if it were the ethical subject.

And the will as a phenomenon is only of interest to psychology.[109]

6.43 If good or bad willing changes the world, it only changes the boundaries of the world, not the facts, not the things that can be expressed in language.

6.431 In death, too, the world does not change but only ceases.

6.4311 Death is not an event in life. Death is not lived through.

If by *eternity* we mean not endless temporal duration but timelessness, then to live eternally is to live in the present.

In the same way as our visual field is without boundary, our life is endless.

6.4312 The temporal immortality of the human soul—its eternal survival after death—is not only without guarantee, this assumption could never have the desired effect. Is a riddle solved by the fact that I survive forever? Is eternal life not as enigmatic as our present one? The solution of the riddle of life in space and time lies *outside* of space and time.

(Certainly it does not involve solutions to any of the problems of natural science.)

6.432   *How* the world is is completely indifferent to what is higher. God does not reveal himself *in* the world.

6.4321   The facts all belong to the setting up of the problem,[110] not to its solution.

6.44   It's not *how* the world is that is mystical, but *that* it is.

6.45   To view the world *sub specie aeterni* is the view of it as a—bounded—whole.

The feeling of the world as a bounded whole is the mystical feeling.

6.5   If the answer cannot be put into words, the question, too, cannot be put into words.

The *riddle* does not exist.

If a question can be put at all, then it *can* also be answered.

6.51   Skepticism is *not* irrefutable, only nonsensical, insofar as it tries to raise doubts about what cannot be asked.

For doubt can only exist provided there is a question; a question can exist only provided there is an answer, and this can only be the case provided something *can* be *said*.

6.52   We feel that even if *all possible* scientific questions were answered, the problems of life would still not have been touched at all. To be sure, there would then be no question left, and just this is the answer.

6.521   The vanishing of this problem is the solution to the problem of life.

(Is this not the very reason why people to whom, after long bouts of doubt, the meaning of life became clear, could not then say what this meaning is?)

6.522   The inexpressible indeed exists. This *shows* itself. It is the mystical.

6.53   The right method in philosophy would be to say nothing except what can be said using sentences such as those of natural science—which of course has nothing to do with philosophy—and then, to show those wishing to say something metaphysical that they failed to give any meaning to certain signs in their sentences. Although they would not be satisfied—they would feel you weren't teaching them any philosophy—*this* would be the only right method.

6.54   My sentences are illuminating in the following way: to understand me you must recognize my sentences—once you have climbed out through them, on them, over them—as senseless. (You must, so to speak, throw away the ladder after you have climbed up on it.)

You must climb out through my sentences; then you will see the world correctly.

7 Of what we cannot speak we must be silent.

Endnotes

1   Compare this to Schopenhauer's assertion, "The world is my idea," which influenced Wittgenstein. The generic and fundamental point is that what the mind has direct access to is not things as they exist independently of the mind (as conceived in materialist metaphysics) but its own items: perceptions, thoughts, and language. For illuminating avatars to Wittgenstein's linguistic variation of the idealistic theme, see the introduction to Berkeley's *Treatise Concerning Human Understanding*, reprinted in my *Mayfield Anthology of Western Philosophy* (Mayfield, 1998), and the related discussion in my *From the Presocratics to the Present: A Personal Odyssey* (Mayfield, 1998). However, we must be careful to note that Wittgenstein is here *not* (at least not straightforwardly) denying the existence of things! If he were, the statements he makes below in which he uses the word "thing" (*ding*) would be the sort of nonsense that Wittgenstein most definitely thinks he is *not* writing, namely, nonilluminating nonsense; for although there is a tension in many of his sentences that, as we shall see, play on contradiction to make their philosophical "showings" clear, it is supposed to be the sort of illuminating "nonsense" that sentences in logic express.

2   Many have thought that this is a mistake. If "one" refers to facts, how can a fact *not* be the case? Others have held that this is not just a mistake, that Wittgenstein is here reverting to an earlier formulation of *Tatsache* as a complex conjunction of elementary, or simple, facts. Thus "It is raining and it is warm" may or may not be the case, whereas "It is warm and it is dark" remain, in his words, "the same." But I think *this* puzzle is solved in the next sentence (2), where he explains what *he* means by fact: facts are not construed in some *standard* type of realism but as "elementary facts" (*Sachverhalten*), such that I think he really meant that any particular *Sachverhalt* may or may not be the case. Indeed, in that regard he talks in 2.06 about positive and negative facts, where a positive fact is the existence of a particular state of affairs and a negative fact is the nonexistence of a particular state of affairs. Thus, for instance, "The Eiffel Tower is taller than Mt. Everest" is a negative fact and "Mt. Everest is taller than the Eiffel Tower" is a positive fact. Finally, 1.21 neatly establishes the distinction between that which Wittgenstein thinks the world is made of—facts—from what common sense says it is made of—things. One major difference between things as ordinarily understood, especially by German-speaking philosophers, is that "If one thing changes its qualities, this can have an effect upon another thing. Things affect each other and resist each one another. . . . This description of things and their interdependence corresponds to what we call the 'natural conception of the world' " (Martin Heidegger, *What Is a Thing?* [South Bend, Indiana: Regnery/Gateway, 1967], p. 33). Notice that here Heidegger, who as much as Wittgenstein but in a different way, is wildly antithetical to any natural conception of the world, nicely and no doubt unintentionally illustrates for us why Wittgenstein would have wanted to insist (and did) that the *world* consisted not of *such* items (things) but of items that are most implicitly *not* linked into a cosmos as conceived in natural science.

3   *Sachverhalt* has been variously translated as "atomic state of affairs," "elementary fact," "atomic fact," and so on. *Particular*, I think, has the better connotation, because the word "atomic" is erroneously ambiguous in that it can mean *both* "something that does not have parts and cannot be further broken down" and "something that consists of [basic] elements." *Particular* would do just as well as "elementary" if we kept in mind the additional sense, "consists of particles," that is, of distinct elements.

4   In translating *Sachverhalt* as "elementary facts," and *Tatsache* as "fact," let us keep in mind what Wittgenstein meant regarding the all-important relation between the two.

Sachverhalt corresponds to a simple declarative sentence if it is true. *Tatsache* corresponds to the totality of all simple declarative sentences when this totality is true. Here is my understanding of this: "Kolak is in his study," is at this moment a true simple declarative sentence. It describes an elementary fact. Likewise, "Kolak is sitting in a chair" is also true. It describes a different elementary fact. "Kolak is writing" is also true and describes yet another elementary fact. These three elementary facts just described using the above three sentences are all related by virtue of a *fact*. It is difficult, perhaps impossible, to say exactly what this fact is, even to specify its boundaries or enumerate it (i.e., count it) in relation to other facts about the world. In an important sense, we don't know of how many facts the world consists because we cannot specify their borders, only the boundary of the world (something that the whole *Tractatus* sets out to delineate). Facts are thus in that sense as elusive to the mind as Kant's things-in-themselves (*ding-an-sich*). However, unlike facts, sentences—which are their linguistic representatives—can be enumerated and there exists the totality of true statements within a language, and so on. So in speaking of elementary facts, Wittgenstein is alluding to the fact that, for instance, it can be observed or seen that Kolak is in his study, sitting in a chair, writing, and so on, elementary facts, all of which can be represented via the content of simple declarative sentences (I just did it), "information bundles" packaged either in linguistic terms (sentences describing observed situations) or experiential terms (items in a visual field). Often, but not always, it may help the understanding to think of "elementary facts" as synonymous to what is available to the perceiving subject in a particular visual field, in terms of the relations of the objects present in that visual field. Indeed, it is in saying that we cannot talk about anything beyond what is present in such elementary facts that Wittgenstein made himself so useful to the logical positivists and members of the Vienna circle. Likewise, it may also sometimes help to think of "elementary facts" as a synonym for *statement*. For a discussion of this sense, in which both visual events and linguistic events can be seen as the mind's "statements to itself" (my terminology, not Wittgenstein's), see below.

5　The original says: *Der Sachverhalt ist eine Verbindung von Gegenständen (Sachen, Dingen).* Clearly, Wittgenstein here means to regard *Ding, Sache,* and *Gegenständ* as synonymous. Clearly, both in ordinary usage as well as in the classical metaphysical implicature, they are not (i.e., the problematic nature of the nature of the relation between [phenomenal] objects to things [in themselves, in Kant's sense). This is not, I think, carelessness on Wittgenstein's part but, rather, merely emphasizes what he conceives to world to *be*. In speaking of x as a *thing,* collection of *things* or *somethings,* and so on, Wittgenstein—like many a philosopher from Kant to Heidegger—is trying to refer to x in the most neutral way possible. "Object" already is specific, it has a direction; the German *Gegenständ* means, literally, "against" (*gegen*) + "stand" (*stand*). That which it stands against is of course the subject, and there is a long philosophical tradition—not just in idealism but in a variety of radical empiricisms, phenomenalisms, and presentationalisms—in which it is held that in order to exist objects as such require a subject. *Thing,* on the other hand, implies therefore something that can stand on its own, independently of being directed at (or, in some views [Fichte's, Schelling's, Schopenhauer's] *from*) a subject. This minimizes one Wittgensteinian tension only to leave us with the problem of how we should then interpret 1.1. Here, however, I think we can help ourselves by helping Wittgenstein to avail himself of straightforward idealism; although Wittgenstein's view of what the world is—like Schopenhauer's—is that the world is, literally, *his* world and no one else's, the items of which it is composed and that stand independently of the ego are not things but facts. And this, again, is to move away from the kind of linkage presented in scientific theories to the unique type of linkage that Wittgenstein is here constructing for us.

So much for the ordinary, pretheoretical sense of these words. Now we turn to the important way in which we shall use certain words in our English rendition of Wittgenstein's *thoughts*, which are often quite clear in the original German without our having to evoke (in this case rather artificial) technical usage. Here it is: the *world* (*Die Welt*) is the totality of *facts* (*Tatsachen*), which consist of *elementary facts* (*Sachverhalten*), which, in turn, consist in configurations of *objects* (*Gegenständen*).

6   This is a perfect example in which I think Wittgenstein uses the word *thing* to emphasize that he is trying to refer to "a something" in as simple and generic way as possible, to mean "a something, an any sort of something," that (in this case) constitutes (is a constituent of) an elementary fact. When he does so in this way, I will, when appropriate, render the thought as simply "something" (as, for instance, in 2.0121).

7   Here the German word is *Sachlage*, which has been translated as "state of affairs," while *Sachverhalt* has been rendered as "*atomic* or *particular* state of affairs." Keeping in mind that, unlike in English, *Sache* (fact, a something), *Tatsache* (fact), *Sachverhalte* (particular states of affairs) and *Sachlage* (state of affairs) all have the word *sach* in common, I have decided on "elementary fact" for both *Sachlage* and *Sachverhalte*. To go beyond that is, in my opinion, mere translational pedantry.

8   How do I know that by "thing" here he means the object, the constituent part of an elementary fact, rather than that he is perhaps presenting a definition of a "thing" in general? Here the section number (2.0122) helps because it tells us that this is a commentary on 2.012, which is itself a commentary on 2.01, which tells us that the things ("the some-things") being talked about are those that make up an elementary fact.

9   Wittgenstein uses the word *form* in several different ways. It can mean *shape*, as in the "form of a spot," *type* or *kind*, as in "form of independence," or *content*, as in "the form of the visual field," or any combination thereof; in the present proposition, for instance, he means all three.

10   The German word *gegeben*, which I have translated as "know," literally means "given, stated, specified." Wittgenstein uses it to mean that something (the object) is referenced through symbolization, such that its existence is implied; that is, the object is expressed in symbolic form.

11   That is, it is symbolized by the value of a variable.

12   For instance, let "Hintikka is wise" be such that Hintikka and wisdom are complexes, then this sentence is analyzable into a statement about the constituents of the concept "Hintikka" and the concept "wisdom" together with a description of these complexes.

13   By the German word *Substanz* (literally, *substance*), Wittgenstein means that which exists independently of what is the case, that is, as what necessarily exists; see 2.024. (The notion has much in common with the German word for reality, *Wirklichkeit*.) First, we must remember: the world is the totality of facts, not things; thus by *substance* (i.e., that which exists independently), he does not mean *matter* but *logical* form, which is for Wittgenstein the most "real" existence (it is permanent, necessary, and unalterable). Furthermore, the reason objects cannot be complex is that if they were, their existence would be contingent and therefore objects could not collectively *be* the reality (substance) of the world. Finally, and perhaps most important, in differentiating between *Wirklichkeit* (reality) and *Welt* (world), the former consists in the existence *and* nonexistence of elementary facts, whereas the world consists only of *existing* elementary facts.

14   That is, if nothing existed necessarily.

15 Think, for instance, of statements in a work of fiction. This, I think, neatly addresses, if it does not solve completely, the problem of the difference between existent and nonexistent objects that has so plagued twentieth-century metaphysics.

16 Here *form* means *content*.

17 That is, what is necessary about the world.

18 By *material properties*, Wittgenstein means "external properties" (see, for instance, 2.0233), in contrast with "formal" or "internal" properties (see 4.122).

19 That is, because objects are without properties, they have neither color nor any other contingent properties. All material, external properties are contingent. This is in spite of the obvious fact that "The apple is red" expresses that something is colored.

20 Here Wittgenstein means that nothing connects the links: the links themselves make connection with one another. That is—and this is a key point—there is nothing in addition to the links, such as glue or solder, that keeps them together; they keep each other together.

21 In other words, the world collectively organized into a coherent whole is reality.

22 The German word *entsprechen*, translated in line with its usual usage as "correspond," has an extremely revealing etymology that accords with Wittgenstein's overall theory: it means, literally, "to speak for." The world speaks. Experiences are its sayings. That's what Wittgenstein has in mind while building his bridge between sentences and facts.

23 I would prefer "speak," but that would move us into a somewhat nonstandard interpretation of Tractarian Objects.

24 A technical note against what has become a commonplace misinterpretation as a result of the Pears-McGuinness translation: the German *sich zu einander verhalten* means "being combined," and so the Pears-McGuinness translation of 2.14 as "What constitutes a picture is that it's elements are related *to one another* in a determinate way," is a paradigm example of how that translation continues to be erroneous and deeply misleading.

25 That is, an *interpreted fact*. And keep in mind that he is not trying to make a point in esthetics about the nature of pictures but, rather, that he is talking about those pictures that we make to ourselves when we picture facts. In other words, he's not informing you about the nature of objects hanging in a gallery but, rather, about the objects hanging inside you and he is using the analogy of pictures of the sort that hang in galleries to make his point.

26 That is, the structure of the fact.

27 That is, the form of the fact.

28 Meaning both the objects depicted and the picture elements that represent them.

29 In other words, it is a standard by which we judge reality.

30 In other words, the representing relation by which it makes contact with reality is, itself, part of the picture. That is, the picture does not need to resemble what it depicts, so that we can somehow depict this resemblance to ourselves. The idea is that nothing stands between our language and our application of that language to the world: they are already in contact.

31 In other words, the meanings (*Bedutungen*) of the elements generate the sense (*Sinn*) of the constitutive object.

32 By *Fuhler* Wittgenstein means, he says, the things that "a butterfly has."

33   Keep in mind that what he means by "fact" is a conglomerate of elementary facts.

34   In other words, the picture's form is a possibility.

35   Compare this with the parallel assertions about sentences, in 4.12 and 4.121, namely, that sentences cannot represent logical form.

36   In other words, because the relation between the picture and what it depicts is external to the picture, the picture can be "true" or "false."

37   In other words, and I think this is key, it is impossible to form a point of view that is independent of any point of view not because that which would be viewed, were such a thing possible, does not exist but because it *does* exist and is *ineffable*. (I have just made a noise directed ostensively at that which Wittgenstein says we must be silent about. Edward Munch's *Silent Scream* comes to mind.)

38   In other words, a picture means something independently of whether it is true or false.

39   By *a priori* proposition he means those whose truth value is determined by their meaning, independently of any comparison with the world.

40   According to Wittgenstein, to think is to form mental pictures.

40.1 If we follow Wittgenstein's numbering plan strictly, this sentence, 3.001, is a fourth-level commentary—explicitly commentary on 3.01. However, 3.01 occurs after 3.001. Furthermore, 3.01, likewise, is a third-level commentary on sentence 3.1, which occurs after 3.01. What I think this shows is not a mistake in Wittgenstein's thinking or numbering system as has sometimes been claimed (see Stenius). Rather, it shows that Wittgenstein is trying, and I think succeeding, to show that this thinking is not linear, that is, it is not strictly speaking in real time.

41   In other words, what is not possible is not thinkable.

42   In Wittgenstein's view, (meaningful) sentences are thoughts expressed in a communicable way.

43   It helps here to think of a projection in geometry, where say a 3-D cube is projected onto a 2-D coordinate system. I think this is an eminently illuminating image that takes us all the way back to Plato's ideal forms, where the relation of an elementary sentence to an elementary fact is like a projective shadow of an ideal form.

44   That is, the form of the possible state of affairs presented.

45   Meaning, it consists of parts connected together in a particular way; that is, the sentence is expressed as a distinct structure. Also, as Wittgenstein himself suggested, "I used the word 'artikuliert' in the sense in which one might say that a man speaks articulate, that is, that he pronounces the words distinctly" (Ludwig Wittgenstein, *Letters to C. K. Ogden*, G. H. von Wright, ed. [Oxford: Basil Blackwell, 1973]).

46   Thus, in *Notes on Logic* he says, "Symbols are not what they seem to be. In *aRb*, *R* looks like a substantive, but it is not one. What symbolizes in *aRb* is that *R* occurs between *a* and *b*. Hence *R* is not the indefinable in *aRb*."

47   Keep in mind that the "world" you presently see around you can be thought of as a pictorial statement—your mind talking to itself with pictures.

48   In mathematical usage, there is the sense of a line or vector, meaning direction; Wittgenstein is here making a play of double meaning.

49 Here I think my earlier point about "speak for" being an illuminating etymological substitute for "correspond" is especially useful.

50 That is, the object signified by the name, the designated object, is the semantic content of the name.

51 That is, symbols.

52 For instance, "The present king of France" is not nonsensical—because there is no present king of France—but merely false. Wittgenstein is here relying on Russell's theory of descriptions.

53 A sentence is indeterminate when we don't know whether the description of the complex refers to anything.

54 Such that it can be used, for instance, as if it were a name for an object.

55 By *primitive sign* (*Urzeichen*) Wittgenstein means one that cannot be defined; so "primitive" is here contrasted with "defined." It is important to keep in mind, however, that his usage once again waxes mathematical, such that which term is primitive, or undefined, and which defined is for the most part a matter of convention. For instance, in geometry we can take a line as the undefined (primitive) and a circle as defined, or start with the circle as undefined and take the line as defined. But since in English this wanes nonsensical, I have chosen (below) to simplify matters and simply use "names" as translation for the cumbersome *Urzeichen,* because that is what Wittgenstein means anyway. See comment below.

56 Thus, names are primitive signs because they have meaning alone and independently. Unlike defined signs, which signify indirectly, a name thus signifies directly.

57 For purposes of elucidation, I have chosen to translate *Urzeichen* not in the literal sense of "primitive signs," which is horribly incoherent English, but as *names,* which is philosophically coherent by Wittgenstein's usage. By my lights, Wittgenstein understands names to be the only primitive signs, as stated clearly in 3.261: "Two signs, one a *Urzeichen* and the other defined by means of *Urzeichen,* cannot signify in the same way. Names cannot be analyzed using definitions."

58 He means that an expression is itself a symbol.

59 Corresponding, roughly, to Russell's "propositional function."

60 For example, if we change "Kolak is a philosopher" to a variable, we get the class of sentences, "x is a philosopher." If we change the constant predicate expression "philosopher" for "man," we get an entirely different type of class of sentences. Now, let us change also the constant into a variable, so we get a class of statements, "x is Y," that are independent of the meanings of the constants in the original sentences. In this way, "x is Y" shows the form of "Kolak is a philosopher."

61 Wittgenstein's conception of *function* is closer to Frege's than to Russell's; Frege considers expressions like 'x is mortal' an expression *for* a function, whereas Russell considers it a propositional function.

62 Now this, of course, can be taken in two different ways, one that I call the conservative, *linguistic* sense and the other that I call the radical, *semiotic* sense: I take 4 in the radical, semiotic sense to mean that—yes—a sentence that makes sense *is* what a thought is; in other words, minds or consciousness as conceived in some superlinguistic (i.e., supernatural) terms are absolutely not required. In my view, the early Wittgenstein, like the

early Russell and Charles Peirce before them both, is intuiting a computational approach to the problem of consciousness, where the computations are logical processes and the items processed are linguistic objects. (Which is not to say that I necessarily agree with it, but only that I think I understand it.)

63   In that they misuse logical syntax.

64   Fritz Mauthner, who rejected the idea of a true logical form and the idea of a perfect language as represented in the symbolism of *Principia Mathematica,* was the first to use the image of the "ladder" which must be thrown away as a simile for language, which Wittgenstein seems to have "borrowed."

65   Literally, "living picture," meaning a sustained pose, a static depiction as with actors on a stage.

66   Notice, however, that it can be shown: he just did it.

67   The famous example of Kant's rose-colored glasses would make everything seem rose-tinted. But we can't imagine glasses that would add a certain sort of spatial relation to an experience where none previously existed. This I would deny; see my lecture to the MIT/Xerox DARC Studio Project "Logic, Space, and Architecture: Implications of Technology." Oct. 3, 1997, MIT, unpublished.

68   Asked by G. E. Moore.

69   This has been erroneously and pejoratively translated as "pseudoconcept," which makes no sense; the contrast is with *proper* and the *Scheinbegriffes* is the same as the formal concept. This is not trivial; what I think Wittgenstein means is that the objects you see presently before you (say, this book) are, literally, concepts illuminated into actual presence by the mind; they are phenomenal and they are a veneer (and, in *that* sense an illusion or a false showing) but one that is ultimately revealing. (One might playfully add, "What cannot be seen must not be looked at.") By *my* lights, I like to think of phenomena as *perceptual notation.*

70   Lewis Carroll's *Alice's Adventures in Wonderland* is a no less wonderful example than is Godel's incompleteness theorem, and I don't think I'm kidding; after all, in his *Notebooks* Wittgenstein says that any words, signs, or symbols that seem to assert something about their own form are *Scheinsatze,* just "like all the sentences of logic." But maybe he thought that he was kidding.

71   Again, I think it would be unphilosophical to take this pejoratively, given what he says about the world being the totality of facts. Now of course the ladder analogy does suggest that everything in the *Tractatus* is nonsense, but once again, it is not like a heap of words that happened to fall together out of a document shredder. It is distinctly illuminating nonsense. And this of course goes double for these comments, which say something about the form of their own form in relation not only to themselves but to what they are about.

72   Again, same comment as above. Many have likened Wittgenstein on such matters as being akin to certain aspects of Zen Buddhist philosophy. Though the Zen Buddhist philosophy is wrong, they are correct, and Wittgenstein is right to say it wrongly so that it can right itself.

73   But notice that there is a ("*non*")sense in which both of those statements are true, in relation to *Scheinbegriffes* such as "2+2 at 3 o'clock equals 7." I.Q.E.D. (*illuminatum quod erat demonstrandum*).

74   He might mean that there is a nondenumerable infinity of them.

75 Thus, writing to his first English translator, Ogden, who translated this locution as "special numbers," Wittgenstein comments:

> What I meant was that in Logic there are no numbers which are in any sense more important or of any greater significance, in any sense preeminent, as compared with the rest of numbers. Such for instance many people believe that the number one is such a number or the number 3. And if—for instance—there was in Logic a definite number of primitive propositions or of primitive ideas—say the number one or any other—then this number would have, in some sense, to *prevail* all through logic and consequently also throughout philosophy. It would then be a number more important than the rest, an "ausgezeichnete Zahl." (*Letters to C. K. Ogden, with Comments on the English Translation of the Tractatus Logico-Philosophicus*, G. H. von Wright, ed. [Oxford: Basil Blackwell, 1973], p. 29).

76 This has often been misunderstood and the cause of much confusion for those who have mistaken Wittgenstein to mean here substitution *salva veritate*, in the same manner as Leibniz in his theory of identity. Rather, Wittgenstein means that the substitution of signs does not alter the sense of the sentences in which the signs occur.

77 That is, have the same semantic content.

78 If we here interpret Wittgenstein to be talking about possible worlds, we thereby counter-invert the state of the *Tractatus* from within Wittgenstein's own world (regarded in its complete form) from the false (as the "later" "Wittgenstein" would "view" it) into the profound.

79 This is the famous "principle of extensionality," as it would later come to be called.

80 In that sense, a truth-table is a declarative sentence. Now, Wittgenstein uses different words—*Satz* (sentence, sometimes translated as "proposition") and *Satzeichen* (literally, sentence sign). In my opinion, this is an unnecessary complication and the source of much confusion, because as far as I can see, their *meaning*, in Wittgenstein's sense of meaning ("the thing meant," that is, the designated object), is *in Wittgenstein's Tractarian the same*. It is not the same in the other philosophies of the time, but I think this just as much confused Wittgenstein, who would have profited much by studying the subsequent work of Church, Gödel, and others.

81 The German *Spielraum* means, literally, "playspace," and one can see here implicitly the seeds of Wittgenstein's subsequent development of what is sometimes dubbed the "game" theory of language.

82 For instance, "It is raining" and "It is raining or it is not raining."

83 Or, one could also speak of their "coordinated objects."

84 This is why, for instance, Ramsey calls tautologies and contradictions "degenerate propositions."

85 I borrow this happy term from Nelson Goodman.

86 Heraclitus speaks; Parmenides is the voice of silence.

87 Another statement of the famous thesis of extensionality.

88 The best way to understand this is with the notion of an index of a set; see any good elementary textbook on topology or set theory. My favorite is Michael C. Gemignani's

Elementary Topology (2nd ed., New York: Dover, 1990), one of those great "Dover paperbacks" that you will find in the math section of any good bookstore and can still buy for only a couple of bucks.

89   Wittgenstein uses the word *enthalten*, which says, literally, that the truth-grounds of *p* are *contained* in the truth grounds of *q*, which is unfortunately confusing; the German expression can be used to say, for instance, "*Wie oft ist 2 in 10 enthalten?*" to ask "How many twos are there in ten?" I think this is how Wittgenstein conceives it in his heart: statements are extracted from facts in the way that numbers are extracted from a number field and so the functional force of sentential logic is enabled through a direct mirroring relation with the facts of which the world in its totality is comprised. On the other hand, on the related matter of what I would call the linguistic extraction of truth from the logical structure of the world, we can by analogy say, "Given that I have 10 things, I have 2 things," "Given that I have 100 things, I have 2 things," and, most perspicuously, "Given that I have $\aleph$ things I have *n* things," where *n* is any number I choose. This, I think, is telling because for Wittgenstein there are in fact $\aleph$ "things" of which the world is comprised, except they are not things but facts. It is, I think, extremely illuminating to conceive the relation of a particular fact to the world in toto as conceptually mirrored in the relation of a particular number, say 3, to $\aleph$. What I particularly like about it is that you cannot in fact remove any number from $\aleph$, and in that sense all numbers are *necessarily* a part of $\aleph$, just as each and every fact is necessarily a part of the world.

90   That is, other than a contradiction or a tautology.

91   Sheffer's stroke, named after its originator, Henry Sheffer. Many have been puzzled by Wittgenstein's (in my view, groundbreaking) assertion about the telling relation between what we might call "symbolic perspicuity" and "proper logical functionality." (Black, for instance, in his commentary says "One can only guess why W. thought the connection between conclusion and premises more 'obvious' in this form than in the alternative notation," and then goes on to speculate: "My best conjecture is that he thought the presence of the stroke function in both premises showed an 'internal connection' which is not so plain when two different logical connectives are used" (Max Black, *A Companion to Wittgenstein's 'Tractatus'* [Ithaca, New York: Cornell University Press, 1964], p. 242). Black, I think, has only scratched the surface. The philosophical profundity lies in the centrality not just in the *Tractatus* but in Wittgenstein's thought in general of the operation, *negation*. It is, I think, a unique point of contact, the blind spot in the mirror, through which the particulars of sentential language and the statements out of which the facts of which the world is made are comprised connect. (The blind spot, after all, is what makes vision possible: it is where the optic "nerve" connects the eye to the brain.) For negation is unique; it is the central black hole in Wittgenstein's negative of the world, in that it not only expresses the common rule for *all logical operations* but is also the foundation for the *general form of truth-function*, the *general form of an operation*, and the *general form of a sentence*. It is respect of the fact that all the immanent forms in Wittgenstein's conception of the world revolve around these general forms, which in turn revolve around the possibility of the universal operation of negation.

92   In other words, sentences that mutually entail each other are identical; this allows him the result that in his ideography all tautologies are identical.

93   Notice the belabored way that he must put this, and for good reason. Why doesn't he say that he can in this way establish that there are the same number of black balls and white balls in the urn? Here we see, I think, a perfect example of what is perhaps most difficult to grasp about Wittgenstein's philosophy, namely, his linguistic idealism. First, notice that

5.154 starts off with "Suppose that . . ." He doesn't just say that's how many are in there, because the question is *what makes it true* that there are a certain number of balls in the urn? In the descriptive context of 5.154, what makes it true is the sentence "Suppose that . . . ," for now we can take it as true what this sentence says. But in the described *reality*, what would make such a sentence true, on my understanding of the Wittgensteinian thesis, is not, say, the arrangement of physical atoms "out there in the world, in the metal container," for those are things that neither language (nor experience) can access. (In that regard, Wittgenstein is a solid breed of Kantian, even as he extends the Kantian thesis into the linguistic domain.) So what "makes" (entails) something (a sentence) to be the case is a *fact*. But "there are an equal number of black balls and white balls" is not a fact but, at best, a particular linguistic representation of a statement. Let us even get on shakier ground and say, as we did before, that a sentence is a linguistic statement. The *observation* that there are an equal number of black balls and white balls in the urn—we take the urn apart and look at all the balls "at once" (loosely speaking, for of course this is not really possible either)— is itself, I have asserted, a type of *statement:* a perceptual statement, an experiential statement, a statement etched not in signs etched with inkblots on paper but in phenomena. Again, this is all to which *we* ever have access. So in 5.154 what is established by Wittgenstein's thought experiment is not something made true by the supposition with which the proposition begins, but something made true by the series of (perceptual and/or linguistic statements) made in drawing out the balls and then remembered according to a schema approximating that used in the method of truth-tables. That is why I think it is correct to say that in the Tractarian World there is no truth independent of statements, and statements are what we use sentences and experiences to present to ourselves. Elsewhere I have expressed this as the thought that what makes a particular proposition true is the propositional framework. See my *In Search of God: The Language and Logic of Belief* (Wadsworth, 1994).

94 That is, fundamental laws.

95 That is, basic concepts.

96 This is exactly what Russell and Whitehead did in sections *9 and *10 *Principia Mathematica* by introducing "~" and "v" all over again for uses with quantifiers. And Quine in section 16 of his *Methods of Logic* introduces them with a truth-functional explanation and then simply goes on to use them in the predicate calculus with what Wittgenstein in 5.452 lampoons as "a perfectly innocent face."

97 A famous saying in Europe, *simplex sigillum veri.*

98 Because the sentence has its form in common with the world.

99 This of course is key: he is realizing here, at this early stage of the game, the fundamental necessity in our ideography of transformation rules, that is, for transforming signs into one another.

100 In other words, "p is possible" is not a picture of an elemental fact.

101 Or "apparent sentences," that is, conglomerates of marks that merely appear to be sentences but really are just marks on paper, noises, etc.

102 This, of course, is not trivial; he has here unpacked one of Hume's most central theses.

103 But let us quickly note that in his *Notebooks* Wittgenstein follows up this sentence immediately with "Physiological life is of course not 'Life.' And neither is psychological life. Life is the world" (77(6)).

104   I agree half-heartedly with Hintikka's contention that what Wittgenstein means by *solipsism* is not *merely* what philosophers usually meant, namely, that there are no other minds besides one's own. (See Hintikka's "On Wittgenstein's 'Solipsism'" [*Mind,* N.S. LXVII, 1958].) That there are no other minds besides my own I take to be a truth not in the limiting sense but in the cosmic sense as perhaps implied by Averroes and others, that all minds are numerically identical beings. (This is a complicated but illuminating notion. See my *I Am You: A Philosophical Explanation of the Possibility That We Are All the Same Person* [Ann Arbor: University of Michigan, 1986] and my *In Search of Self: Life, Death and Personal Identity* [Wadsworth, 1998].) Stenius, too, agrees with Hintikka, "at least in so far as Wittgenstein ought to have used the word 'idealism' rather than 'solipsism,' because what he calls 'solipsism' is exactly his linguistic turn of Kantian idealism," (Erik Stenius, *Wittgenstein's Tractatus: A Critical Exposition of Its Main Lines of Thought* [Ithaca, N.Y.: Cornell University Press, 1964]). I say "half-heartedly" not because I do not fully agree with Hintikka (I would not dare) but because I *more* than agree with him: I think Wittgenstein (whether he consciously realized it or not) meant *both* the (linguistic turn of) Kantian (transcendental, or critical) idealism and the cosmic "there are no other minds but mine" truth.

105   He says "transcendental," but I think this is a mistake; he means *transcendent.* See my comment regarding the ethical, in endnote 108.

106   Once again, this is not meant pejoratively.

107   Bertrand Russell added this comment in his notes: "i.e., not the form of one particular law, but of any law of a certain sort."

108   He says "transcendental" but this is a mistake; he means "transcendent." Transcendental is used both by Kant and Wittgenstein (but by neither always consistently) to mean the limits of theoretical knowledge as known by reaching beyond experience not outside the mind but into the inner workings of the mind, via the categories and forms of perception and thought. Transcendent refers to what exists beyond that limit, not on the inside but outside, beyond the categories of thought, "outside the mind" (such as Kant's things-in-themselves). For further clarifications on this fundamental point, see the sections of Kant and Wittgenstein in my *From the Presocratics to the Present* (Mayfield, 1998), my *Lovers of Wisdom* (Wadsworth, 1997), and my *In Search of Kant* (Wadsworth, 1998).

109   That is, that it seems people's intentions obviously affect the course of events is merely an appearance, a phenomenon, of superficial psychological interest, without any philosophical significance.

110   In German, *Aufgabe* refers to trivial elementary school exercises, such as spelling, multiplication tables, and so on—an expression of which Wittgenstein was extremely fond.